*To the memory of
my brother and friend, Nosn,
who died a hero's death
in the Warsaw ghetto.*

The author

Jews Without Yellow Stars
Stories of Jewish Partisan Fighters in Occupied Belarus

By Hersh Smolar

Translated by Ruth Murphy

Edited by Catherine Madsen

With an Introduction by
Dr. Solon Beinfeld

Ben Yehuda Press
Teaneck, New Jersey

Jews Without Yellow Stars ©2024 **Ruth Murphy.** All rights reserved. No part of this book may be used or reproduced in any manner whatsoever without written permission except in the case of brief quotations embodied in critical articles and reviews.

Published by Ben Yehuda Press
122 Ayers Court #1B
Teaneck, NJ 07666
http://www.BenYehudaPress.com

To subscribe to our monthly book club and support independent Jewish publishing, visit https://www.patreon.com/BenYehudaPress

Ben Yehuda Press books may be purchased at a discount by synagogues, book clubs, and other institutions buying in bulk. For information, please email markets@BenYehudaPress.com

ISBN13 978-1-963475-51-7 paper   978-1-963475-52-4 epub

Cover photo of Belarus partisans courtesy of Shoshana Razel Gordon Guedalia, whose grandfather, Pesach Paul Brem, of Lida, is top left. Colorized by Photoshop. Back cover photo features Hersh Smolar on the upper right. Colorized by Photoshop. Full caption on page 54.

Permissions and Acknowledgements

"The Family" was published in Issue 36, April 2024 of the JewishFiction.net website. Earlier versions of "The Family" and "Resurrection of the Dead" (Vol. 27, Issue 2, Fall 2019) and "Night of the White Devils" and "The President of our Capital" (Vol. 28, Issue 2, Fall 2020) were published in *Metamorphoses*, the journal of the Five College Faculty Seminar for Literary Translation.

Ex Libris plate on page 121 from an article by E. Getmansky in the magazine-newspaper *Workshop* (Мастерская). Published with the kind permission of the editor.

24 25 26 / 10 9 8 7 6 5 4 3 2 1   20240809

TABLE OF CONTENTS

Translator's Note	vii
General Historical Notes	x
Introduction to *Jews Without Yellow Stars*	xiii
In Place of a Preface	1
Foreword to the 1952 Edition	6
A Good Morning!	8
T'khies Hameysim (Resurrection of the Dead)	11
Under the Ground	16
Certainty	21
At the Edge	25
The Last Letters	28
A Night in the Forest	30
Right Inside the Ghetto	33
The Red-headed Miller	36
The Debt Made Good	38
The Concert	42
Partisan Bookkeeping	47
The Family	55
The Night of the White Devils	60
His Machine Gun	70
Enemies	74
The Judgment	80
The Czech Rifle	84
The President of Our Capital	89
Old Shimen Tells a Tale	94
The Password	98
The Issue is Ready for Print	102
With Compass in Hand	108

By a Special Means	113
No Longer an Orphan	116
The "Deserter"	122
The First "Quintet" of the Budyonni Detachment	127
"I Have a Little Boy"	132
The Nurse	138
With the Enemy's Bomb	141
The Third Bridge	145
The End and the Beginning	151
The 14-Year-Old Flagbearer	155
With the Same Hands	159
Appendix: 10 December 1942	163
Bibliography	176
Acknowledgements	181
About the Author	182
About the Translator	183
About the Editor	183

TRANSLATOR'S NOTE

Hersh Smolar was a well-known writer in multiple languages, and the spelling of his name varies from language to language. I have chosen to use the English spelling: Hersh Smolar. His name also appears as Grzegorz Smolar (Polish), and the Yiddish spelling of his last name (סמאָליאַר) is Smoliar (pronounced Smol-yar). His brother's name in Yiddish is Nosn Smoliar, with the English spelling Natan Smolar.

Paradoxically, the two hardest words to translate in Smolar's stories were two very simple words: *opteyl* and *opteylung*. These two words seem to have identical meanings; Smolar uses one word or the other, over and over, to designate partisan fighting units, sometimes using both words in the same paragraph, and once even in the same sentence. Whether he had a different meaning or nuance in mind for each word, or whether it was simply a stylistic choice, I have no idea. I translated them as best I could in the context of the story, and from what I know of WWII Jewish and Soviet partisan units. For the most part, I've chosen to use the word "detachment" for both *opteyl* and *opteylung*. I've kept the general convention of referring to most of the better-known Jewish partisan groups as "Detachment" (e.g., "106th Detachment").

A further issue complicating the translation of these two words is that there really is no good equivalent in the modern English lexicon, military or otherwise. English military vocabulary during WWII isn't a good fit, because there is really no equivalence between these partisan units and more standardized traditional military groups. Jewish partisan groups were extremely fluid in both size and membership. Faced with vicious anti-Semitism from other partisan groups—even Soviet groups, although officially the Soviets discouraged it—Jewish partisans would form their own groups which were sometimes strictly fighting groups, sometimes family groups with a core fighting unit. These groups would grow in size (or be destroyed) and then often split off again and/or be absorbed into existing Soviet bands. With no good way to define them, I simply stayed with the translation mentioned above.

Another source of confusion was Smolar's use of the word *blockade* ("blockade") in several stories (see "Mit der soyne's bombe/With the Enemy's Bomb"), referred to as "marathons." By description they were not traditional blockades, but actually assaults that first encircled and then attacked partisan bases. We also see this term in Nosn Smolar's testimony in Appendix I, where again he appears to be describing encirclements and then assaults, rather than a conventional blockade.

Smolar uses tense very fluidly in his stories, often switching from past to present and back to past again within several paragraphs. The Yiddish language allows this and it works quite well, but English is not so flexible. I've chosen for the most part to stay in the past tense, occasionally retaining the present to preserve the vividness and feeling of action in the scene.

I've also tried to preserve as much of Smolar's original Yiddish as possible, following mainly the 1948 edition. In the bilingual text, I've corrected only obvious printing errors and spelling differences that might cause confusion to the reader. I've left the spelling of names and places in the Yiddish, noting the Belarussian names in the Historical Notes whenever possible.

In some cases, the 1952 edition clarifies confusing passages in the 1948 edition. I have not specifically noted these in each story, but simply made the corrections.

All translations in the text and citations are mine, unless otherwise indicated.

Abbreviations for Books by Hersh Smolar
[Written in Yiddish as *Smoliar*]

FMG	*Fun minsker geto*
RM	*Resistance in Minsk*
SY	*Sovetishe yidn hinter geto-tsoymen*
TMG	*The Minsk Ghetto: Soviet-Jewish Partisans Against the Nazis*
VBK	*Vu bistsu khaver Sidorov?*

Citations of other authors will be in standard format, by last name.

GENERAL HISTORICAL NOTES

Of all the occupied ghettos during WWII, the Minsk ghetto was unique in the astounding number of Jews—approximately ten thousand—who were able to escape to the surrounding forests, between the time of the ghetto's establishment in July 1941 and liquidation in October 1943. This was due to diverse factors, including terrain, the geographical and political history of Byelorussia and its Jewish populations, the proximity of the Soviet Union, and the status of Minsk as a Soviet-occupied city at the time of the German invasion.

Smolar's decision to enter the Minsk ghetto was a significant factor in the successful development of an efficient underground movement, one that was able first to build relationships with the local partisan groups, and eventually to create an independent group. He was, as Evgeny Finkel writes, "a high-ranking activist with decades of underground work under his belt." A communist, he linked up with other trusted communist cadres. By August 1941, a Jewish underground was created, led by Smolar (Finkel 2017, 165). By 1942, he had escaped the Minsk ghetto, fleeing to the nearby Naliboki forest, where he became a commissar in a partisan brigade and helped organize the many Soviet partisan units (Tec 1993, 265). His importance in creating and sustaining a well-run underground movement in the ghetto, along with the emergence of Jewish partisan groups, cannot be emphasized enough. Without his experience and leadership, things might have gone very differently.

The forests around Minsk held various partisan units that continuously interacted with each other, particularly as most came under Soviet control (Tec 1993, 126). As a partisan leader, Smolar had relationships with the many units, including a warm one with the Bielski brothers' brigade. Both were dedicated to saving Jews and leading as many as possible out of the ghettos. Tec notes that "Smolar was very helpful to Tuvia Bielski. His high position in the Soviet partisan movement gave Tuvia protection, particularly with General Platon," who headed up the Soviet partisans for the Baranowicze region (Tec 1993, 265).

The Jews of Minsk created the 406, Kutuzov, Budyonny, Dzerzhinskiy, Sergei Lazo, and Parkhomenko Detachments, as well as the 106th Family Detachment, which provided protection in the forests for over 600 Jewish women and children (Roth 1971, 55). Both the Parkhomenko Detachment (part of the Chapaev Brigade) and the 106th Detachment were well-known Jewish partisan groups. Many of the Jews who escaped from the Minsk and other local ghettos became part of this group.

The 106th Detachment, known as "Zorin's brigade," commanded by Sholem (Simkhe) Zorin, ultimately consisted of 558 people, only one of whom was not Jewish (a Byelorussian). It included 137 fighters, 16 of whom were women. It also held 421 unarmed women, children, and elderly people. The brigade produced shoes and clothing, operated a bakery, laundry and hospital, and protected itself by moving deeper into the forest. Epstein writes, "Other than some casualties among the fighters in the last months, Zorin's Brigade survived the war intact" (Epstein 2008, 23-24).

Children were valued members of these groups, as well as in the ghetto underground, serving as guards, spies, forest guides, scouts, and messengers. Pulling out a ball and feigning play, they could keep watch during clandestine meetings without arousing suspicion. "Zorin and other partisan commanders relied on children because of their ability to slip in and out of the ghetto, their excellent memories, and their lack of fear. Children from the ghetto often knew its layout and the various places where one could enter or leave it better than adults. They quickly learned the routes to the forest and were aware of every point of danger along those routes" (Tec 2008, 215-216). Smolar's 1952 version of this text contains four stories honoring these children (some as young as nine) and their extraordinary intelligence, calm and courage.

Toward the end of his time as a partisan, Smolar was part of a shared command of the Komsomolski brigade. Along with two Russians as commandant and commissar, Smolar served as the political chief, in charge of the brigade propaganda and communications (Tec 2003, 330).

INTRODUCTION TO

JEWS WITHOUT YELLOW STARS

By Solon Beinfeld

This collection of sketches of partisan life in Belarus during the German occupation (1941-1944) introduces us to a moment of particular historical interest. It deals with a particular time and place, but also stresses the Jewish participation in the partisan struggle. Above all, it represents the experience, the outlook and the hopes of its author, Hersh Smolar (1905-1993). The Yiddish original was first published in Lodz in 1948, at a time when Warsaw was largely still in ruins. A revised and expanded addition appeared in Warsaw in 1952. Some of the sketches had already appeared in Smolar's memoir, *Fun Minsker Geto* (Moscow, 1946), a rare example of Soviet Jewish Holocaust literature, which was translated into Russian and sold tens of thousands of copies.

Partisan activity in Belarus during World War II was greatly celebrated in Soviet historiography. Indeed Belarus, with its dense forests and swamps, stands out among other German-occupied areas for the strength and duration of its partisan movement. The notion of the "Partisan Republic" of Belarus was propagated as an outstanding example of the true unity of Party and People during the Great Patriotic War. Jewish participation in this most intense partisan war, vividly described by Smolar, soon faded from the Soviet writings about the War. Even western historiography has mainly seen Jewish partisans primarily as refugees who set up "family camps" (like the one of the famous Bielski brothers) essentially for survival, although in a few cases, as in the case of the Bielski family camp, they also became an active partisan base. But in Smolar's sketches we have a complex and balanced picture in which Jews do sometimes appear as refugees, but primarily as fighters—very significant in the struggle in and around Minsk. This history is now being made available to a wider public. To understand how Smolar presents the Jewish fighters simultaneously as nationally conscious Jews and as true Soviet partisans, we need to examine Smolar's life—before, during and after the Second World War.

Smolar was born in 1905 in Zambrow, in what is now western Belarus but was then a part of Czarist Russia. He was exposed early in life to the socialist and revolutionary ideas which circulated among Russian Jews in the years leading up to the First World War and the Russian Revolution. In the aftermath of the War, Zambrow was contested between two post-war regimes—the Polish Republic and Soviet Russia. The city ultimately became part of Poland, but during the time that Soviet troops temporarily occupied the city in 1920 Smolar had his first taste of Communist rule and also his first experience of Communist activism and leadership, despite his extreme youth. After the Polish victory, Smolar chose not to remain in Poland, but fled to Soviet Russia, beginning his career as a dual Polish and Soviet Jewish activist. He had become convinced that Communism was the answer to the so-called Jewish Question.

In those years, the 1920s, that conviction had much to support it. The Soviet regime had put an end to the vicious pogroms of 1919-21 and given Yiddish, the language of the masses, official recognition in education and literature. Yiddish was one of the four official languages of Belarus, along with Belarussian, Russian and Polish. There were even Yiddish-language courts. Jewish agricultural settlements multiplied in Crimea and within the former Pale of Settlement. In 1928, Birobidjan, in the Soviet Far East, was designated as an area reserved for Jewish settlement and the eventual establishment of an autonomous Jewish region. Smolar was active in Jewish institutions in Kiev (Kyiv) and other cities, then settled in Moscow where he was enrolled in the Yiddish Section of the Comintern (Communist

International) University for Western Peoples, which prepared young people for activism outside the Soviet Union. In 1928, after declining to go to Palestine, he was sent as a Comintern agent to Poland, where the Communist party was illegal. He was active in Poland in labor and agricultural strikes and protests, rather than in specifically Jewish affairs. He was twice arrested, and was in prison in Brest-Litovsk when the Second World War broke out.

Germany invaded Poland on 1 September 1939. The Soviet Union followed suit on 17 September. With the collapse of the Polish state, Smolar made his way to Bialystok, in the Soviet-occupied zone, eager to undertake Jewish activism there. Locked away in jail in Poland, he had avoided the Soviet purges of the 1930s, which had claimed the lives of a number of Yiddish writers and cut short much of the Soviet-Jewish activity. The Yiddish-language schools were closed and even the Birobidjan project was seriously undermined. This policy, however, did not extend to the newly-annexed Polish territories, where clericalism and capitalism had to be fought in the language of the Jewish masses. Smolar could thus return to Soviet territory with his idealism intact. Bialystok became a hub of Soviet Jewish activity and Smolar was appointed the Secretary of the Bialystok Yiddish daily, *Der Bialistoker Shtern*, the main Yiddish newspaper in the region. The newspaper followed the Party line, roundly denouncing Judaism, non-Communist Jewish parties, and the bourgeois Jewish elite, while keeping silent about what was happening to Polish Jews across the border under German rule. But it did provide a visible Yiddish presence in what was now part of Soviet Belarus.

This stage of Smolar's life came to an abrupt end when the Germans invaded the Soviet Union on 22 June 1941. Bialystok, close to the border, was overrun within days. Smolar saw to it that the walls of the city were plastered with the last issue of *Der Bialistoker Shtern*. Many journalists and writers were evacuated to the interior of the Soviet Union, but Smolar declined to go along, instead heading for Minsk on foot, hoping he could be part of the anti-fascist struggle in the defense of Minsk, the capital of Belarus. But the Soviets had fled by the time Smolar arrived. He found the city undefended and leaderless. The Germans arrived soon after. As they did everywhere, they herded the remaining Jews (at least 70,000 people) into a ghetto. They forced all Jews to sew yellow stars onto their clothes, which was later recalled as a particularly painful experience. In the story "Partisan Bookkeeping," the wounded Jewish partisan tells the medical student who had become a "doctor" in the ghetto and must operate on him, not to fear cutting deeper—it won't hurt as much as sewing on the yellow star.

Thus began the chapter of Smolar's life that is bound up with the fate of the Jews of the Minsk ghetto. In his postwar memoirs, Smolar points out the special character of the Minsk ghetto, compared to other Nazi ghettos. It was the largest ghetto within the boundaries of the pre-1939 Soviet Union. Unlike Vilna or Bialystok, cities only recently Soviet-occupied, Minsk contained a fully Soviet Jewish population. This population, especially its youth, had for a generation been in close contact with the non-Jewish population and a full participant in Soviet civic life. Even physically, the ghetto stood out: it was not surrounded by a wall, or a high fence, but by barbed wire, which could be cut. Not far from Minsk were vast forests and swamps that facilitated partisan activity. It was also true that the local non-Jewish population of Eastern Belarus was not antisemitic to the same extent as, for example, the Ukrainians or the Poles, nor did it resent the Jews for their support of the Soviet occupation, as did, for example the Lithuanians, many Poles and even Western Belarussians. Indeed, the Nazis had trouble recruiting Belarussians to assist them in carrying out mass shootings, and Lithuanian volunteers had to be brought in. Nazi officials complained that the local Belarussians did not seem to grasp the "racial" aspects of the anti-Soviet struggle.

The Jews of the newly-created Minsk ghetto had been, like all Soviet Jews, unaware of the nature of Nazi persecution of Jews in Poland. Such information had been withheld during the period of the Ribbentrop-Molotov Pact. Some even felt the ghetto would provide a certain amount of security and solidarity. But the Minsk ghetto quickly learned the real meaning of German rule. Shootings and deportation to killing sites began almost immediately and never stopped. Unlike some other ghettos, the Minsk ghetto had no period of relative stability. *Aktionen*[1] (*Aktsyes* in Yiddish), German anti-Jewish operations, were relentless, beginning with the mass execution of intellectuals in November 1941. Some, like the so-called *Purim Aktsye* of March 1942, were particularly bloody; killings eventually reduced the population of the ghetto to 9,000 at the time of its liquidation in October 1943. Underground activity in the Minsk ghetto began early. Smolar, a veteran of illegal activity, was one of its founders and leaders. In Warsaw, Bialystok and elsewhere, the emphasis was on resistance and revolt within the ghetto itself. In Minsk, it was decided that resistance within the ghetto was futile, apart from sabotage and theft of weapons. The non-Jewish resistance within Minsk itself was quicky crushed, leaving the ghetto resistance on its own. Under those circumstances, only leaving the ghetto and joining and finding refuge among the partisans was meaningful.

Over time, thousands of Jews were led to safety in this way, a unique phenomenon in the history of Nazi ghettos. Minsk ghetto Jews had in their favor the proximity of relatively friendly partisan territory (except where the antisemitic Polish Armia Krajowa operated). The ghetto population had to be informed of this; hence the need for a literal underground press, as described in "Under the Ground." The Soviet partisan leadership also had to be persuaded that the rescue of Jews was not just a moral obligation, but also a practical necessity in fighting the Germans. Minsk Jews had many connections in a region they knew well. Many had useful skills and some Jews, as recounted in "Old Shimen Tells a Tale," had previous partisan experience from the civil war period. In a relatively short time, the ghetto became a center not only of conventional acts of resistance, but more importantly a movement to evacuate the largest possible number of people from the ghetto and lead them to the partisans.

The first *Judenrat* (Jewish Council), the nominal ghetto authority created by German order, was fully aligned with the resistance, a

---

1. Massacres of Jewish populations by the German military or police, involving mass assembly, deportation and slaughter.

stance for which its members were later executed. The Jewish Ghetto Militia (Police) was infiltrated by the Resistance and was not, as in other ghettos, always despised as a collaborationist force. Yes, some were thugs like those described in "The Resurrection of the Dead," who would check for Jews who were avoiding labor duty. But even labor duty was not always a death sentence; depending on where one was sent, it could be an opportunity for resistance. In the Minsk ghetto, as in other ghettos, Jews fit for labor and forced to work for German or collaborationist workshops were temporarily spared execution. Under escort, they marched outside the ghetto to their workplaces. This enabled them to gather information, sometimes from their German employers, and bring news to the ghetto, their reports eagerly awaited, as described in "Security." In addition, the crowding and confusion at the ghetto gate as labor units marched out was one way to leave the ghetto and escape to the forest.

The close links between the ghetto and the partisans meant for Smolar that the identity of Jewish and Communist interests had been achieved and is repeatedly emphasized in these sketches. As the title of the book suggests, joining the partisans represented liberation for the inmates of the ghetto, enabling them to remove the yellow badges of shame. At the same time, Jews were an important element in the makeup of the partisan units. There were units that were entirely Jewish until they merged with other forces. Overall, Jews were a minority of the partisans, but a substantial and visible one. In "The Password," Smolar describes how the Brigade's Intelligence officer, prone to devising complicated passwords taken from quotations by Pushkin or Lermontov, also shared quotations from Sholem Aleichem (in Russian translation) with his Jewish partisan deputy. Jews who had military experience were naturally welcome, as were those with an intimate knowledge of the landscape. In "His Machine Gun," Khayim Aleksandrovich takes part in an attack on the German garrison in a town where there is also a small ghetto. The attack destroys the garrison and at the same time frees the Jews. The young among them join the partisans, and the rest are led to family camps and later smuggled across the front lines. Even Jews without military experience could contribute to the moral level of the unit. In the touching story "The President of Our Capital," Brigade Commander Vasilevski appoints as his Adjutant Tevl, the ex-Yeshiva student so respected in the community that even peasants came to him with their disputes. Conversing with Tevl helps Vasilevski to think deeply, and at the same time the unmilitary Tevl (and by implication other Jews) is protected from ridicule. Even Jews who kept kosher as best they could (eating only onions!) and piously reluctant to display their deadly weapons openly, very much keeping to themselves (as described with evident sympathy in "The Family"), were accepted.

This is not to say that there was never friction between Jews and non-Jews. Vasilevski's motives hint at this. Some units were reluctant to receive Jewish refugees. Some non-Jewish partisans alleged that Jews only looked out for other Jews. In turn, Jews could be suspicious of their non-Jewish fellow-partisans. In "The Debt Made Good," Commander Dakhno asks the Jewish partisan Pogarelits why Jews are avoiding his unit. The reason, it turns out, is that he is the grandson of the Ukrainian Anarchist Nestor Makhno, whose bands during the civil war era were accused by the Soviets spokesmen of carrying out pogroms against the Jewish population (which he denied). His grandson has to repay his family's "debt" by blowing up a German train, an action in which he is killed. Pogarelits is then named in his place. On the whole, it appears, relations between Jewish and non-Jewish partisans remained amicable.

The role of Jewish women and children in the partisan movement is of great interest to Smolar. Women asserted their rights to be treated as equal fighters. In "The Czech Rifle," Tsilye holds on to the weapon she had stolen from the Germans back in Minsk when she arrives at the partisan base. She clings to it despite suggestions that her proper role is cooking and cleaning. She uses the rifle during a successful attack on a German train (but Smolar describes her as a good cook anyway). In "The Nurse," a woman with experience as a pharmacist arrives from the Minsk ghetto to serve as a nurse. When the base is moved, the old and sick have to be left behind. The nurse insists on remaining with them and continuing to care for them. In "The Judgment," a Jewish woman, who arrived at the base carrying her dead child, is silently resentful at being relegated to cooking and laundering. When German prisoners are brought to the base, no longer silent, she savagely attacks a German prisoner, for which she must be tried. "'I Have a Little Boy,'" whose title derives from a famous poem by Morris Rosenfeld, expresses a woman's role from a different perspective. A Jewish woman, Liube, pregnant and distraught, appeals to the base commander for help. Pregnancy was generally a liability for women partisans, but in this story the commander refuses to summon the doctor for an abortion, saying Jews should not assist the Germans in destroying them. He offers Liube a lighter workload and she later gives birth to twins, a sign that the Jewish people will live on.

Jewish children, especially boys, are described in several stories as essential participants in the partisan movement. With their knowledge of the region and their contacts from their *Komsomol* and school days with Belarussian boys and their families, they made for excellent scouts and guides. In "No Longer an Orphan," 12-year-old Vilik has made the resistance his family. He leads groups out of the Minsk ghetto and goes back and forth between the ghetto and the forest. In "With Compass in Hand," young Yoshke, a recent arrival from the ghetto who has not yet learned the manners of the base, undergoes a harsh form of hazing when the detachment commander orders an even younger boy to get him lost in the frigid nighttime forest and then "rescue" him. Perhaps the most dramatic account of the role of the young is to be found in "The Night of the White Devils." A group of youths (from nine to 14 years of age) are assigned to keep watch on the base while the adult partisans are off on an operation. They become bored with just sitting there and decide to take off on their own. They successfully raid a local Belarussian police base and return with captured horses, cows and sheep. They have thereby disobeyed orders and must be punished. Their "punishment" is two weeks of kitchen duty, but thereafter they are considered true partisans.

Smolar describes partisan life from his own experiences, but he did not join the partisans right away. He remained in the Minsk ghetto as long as he could, as a leading figure in the underground, for over a year. He evaded capture by the Germans (who had his name and a number of aliases on their list) by various stratagems, including hiding in the ghetto infirmary. But after the *Aktionen* of July 1942 he decided he had done what he could in helping others leave the ghetto. It was now time for him to leave the ghetto himself (August 1942). He joined a Jewish partisan unit already established in the forests, which eventually merged with the larger partisan establishment. He was not only a high-ranking fighter, but also a commissar and the editor of the partisan newspaper, similar to the one described in "The Issue is Ready to Print."

That the Soviet partisans and the Jews were united in their struggle against the common fascist enemy is a major theme for Smolar. But underlying it is the idea that Jews had an additional motive—that of revenge for their murdered families. This notion appears in multiple sketches, where Jewish combatants keep a special kind of "score," killing enemy soldiers to match their murdered families. For Smolar, therefore, the Jews were the ultimate partisans and as such were accepted by the non-Jews who fought alongside them.

With the victorious outcome of the war and the partisan struggle, Smolar had reason to hope that the future of Jewish culture would be secure despite the loss of so much of the Jewish population. During the war, there had been a revival of sorts. The Jewish Antifascist Committee was founded in the Soviet Union to influence Jewish opinion abroad (its visit to the United States in 1943 created a sensation) and had become a quasi-official representation of Soviet Jewry. It had as its voice a new Yiddish daily, *Eynikayt* (Unity), which began appearing in 1942. (The pre-war daily *Emes* (Truth) had ceased publication in 1938). The faltering Birobidjan project was renewed at the end of the war as a destination for survivors of devastated Jewish communities. There was even (very risky) talk within the Jewish Antifascist Committee of a more accessible Jewish autonomous region in Crimea, where Jewish settlements existed before the war and which was now depopulated since the local Tatars were deported as "collaborators." Thus in 1946 the wartime revival seemed to have continued into the postwar period. But, as it turned out, Smolar's memoir of the Minsk ghetto was more of a last gasp. It was issued not long before all Soviet Yiddish publication and culture, including all references to Jews as partisans or even as victims of the Nazis, came to an abrupt end. Just as Smolar had avoided the purges of the 1930s while in Polish jails, so he now avoided, in the nick of time, the brutal suppression of Soviet Jewish life by being sent back to Poland. For a while he remained in contact with the Jewish Antifascist Committee, speaking with one of its leading members, Itsik Fefer, by phone once a week. But when he was told that Fefer no longer could be reached by phone and learned that the Jewish Antifascist Committee had been dissolved as unnecessary once the war was over, Smolar understood that things were not going well in the Soviet Union. He could not yet know the full extent of anti-Jewish policy—that Fefer and the rest of the Jewish Antifascist Committee, along with other Jewish activists, had been arrested and were ultimately to be executed. Despite the worrisome scene in the Soviet Union, Smolar felt that Poland (by then a Communist state) offered an alternative.

Nonetheless, Jewish life in Poland could not compare with its prewar vibrancy. Relatively few Jews had survived. Even the survivors, indeed even the returnees from the Soviet Union, tended to leave the country, often for Displaced Persons (DP) Camps in the US sector of Germany and then for Israel. Still, there were serious attempts to revive Jewish life, though non-Communist groups like the Bund and the Zionists were not tolerated for long. Some projects—like creating a Jewish autonomous district in former German Silesia—were bound to fail. Nevertheless, a relatively robust Jewish life was permitted and even encouraged. This "*Nusekh Poyln,*" the special Polish version of Jewish life under Communism, included Yiddish publishing (e.g., both versions of *Jews Without Yellow Stars*, the Lodz 1948 and the Warsaw 1952) and a celebrated Yiddish theater under the direction of the noted actress Ida Kaminska. Politically, a Central Committee of Polish Jews was created, of which Smolar became head. Above all, there was a daily Yiddish newspaper, *Di Folks-Shtime*, for which Smolar served as one of the editors. He hoped that the Polish example might eventually influence Soviet policy. None of the Polish Jewish institutions had a counterpart in the Soviet Union. Soviet Jews had limited contact with the outside world, even Communist Poland, but the Warsaw newspaper managed to reach some individuals. Soviet Yiddish writers, who had no outlet (until 1961 and the inauguration of *Sovetish Heymland*), could on occasion be published in *Di Folks-Shtime*.

Di Folks-Shtime had of course to follow the Party line, but Smolar became more and more uneasy about the fate of the members of the Jewish Antifascist Committee members, which remained a mystery. With the death of Stalin in 1953, Smolar could hope for a return to the "pure" Communism of Lenin, but it was not until Khrushchev's "secret" speech before the 20th Congress of the Communist Party of the USSR in February 1956 that it became possible to contemplate and even demand answers. Soon enough, Smolar learned the terrible truth. An American correspondent, Leon Crystal of the New York Yiddish *Forward*, while on his way home from Moscow, stopped off in Warsaw and visited *Di Folks-Shtime*. There he passed on what he had learned from the Israeli Embassy in Moscow about the arrest and execution in August 1952 of the members of the Jewish Antifascist Committee and other Jewish cultural figures. The Israeli government preferred not to announce its findings directly. Smolar knew and trusted Crystal and decided it was time to act. The report in the *Forward* could be denounced as malicious slander, but the same news in a Communist newspaper in Poland would have an entirely different impact. The article, unsigned but known to be by Smolar, appeared in *Di Folks-Shtime* on April 4, 1956, entitled *"Undzer veytik un undzer treyst"* ("Our Sorrow and Our Consolation"), was an immediate sensation. It mentioned the executed writers and actors, some of whom were world-famous, by name. That was Smolar's "sorrow." His "consolation" was that with the passing of Stalin and Beria, there could be a new birth of Soviet Jewish life. But despite the *pro forma* optimism, the article was damning. It had an impact on Jewish and non-Jewish leftists worldwide. As a result, *Di Folks-Shtime* was effectively banned from the Soviet Union. (A personal note: In 1959, as a student visiting Moscow, I noticed that the hotel newspaper kiosk had Communist newspapers from around the world except Yiddish ones. When I asked the clearly Jewish kiosk attendant for the Warsaw *Folks-Shtime*, he led me behind the kiosk and in a hushed Yiddish conversation asked about Israel and expressed his desire to go there.) As late as 1967, the *Folks-Shtime*, unlike other Communist newspapers, could accurately describe the Israeli victory in the Six Day War, but by then Smolar's position on the paper and in all Polish Jewish institutions had become untenable and he was fired from all his positions.

After the brutally antisemitic Gomulka campaign of 1968-69, which severely affected the remaining Jews of Poland, causing many of them to leave, Smolar decided finally that Jews and Communism were not compatible, even in Poland. He left for Paris and then for Israel, feeling at last at home there with his people. In his extensive later writings and in his lengthy filmed interview with Claude Lanzmann for *Shoah*, Smolar renounces Communism altogether. In his final years, he wrote extensively and critically about his experiences with the *Yevsektsiya* (the Jewish Section of the Soviet Communist Party until its liquidation in 1930) and other moments in his long career. For him and for history, the ideal of Jewish Communism was a dream. But the special moment when Jews removed their yellow stars and fought as Soviet partisans was a reality that deserves to be remembered.

Solon Beinfeld is Professor Emeritus of History at Washington University in St. Louis, and Co-Editor-in-Chief of the Comprehensive Yiddish-English Dictionary *(Bloomington, Indiana University Press, 2013).*

Jews Without Yellow Stars

In Place of a Preface

The only one who was worried was Myetshislav Kozak, who sat there and from time to time in a monotone, with typical peasant obstinacy, repeated:

"To hell with this whole game...."

"Why are you so worked up about it, old beggar? What, like it's the first time? How many times already have we scoured ourselves down to the skin, made our faces 'respectable,' when the need arose?"

The perpetually grumpy Marilya Jekon was, this time, in an unexpectedly cheerful mood. What hadn't she already been faced with having to do in her lifetime, this Polish woman from the Dambrov coal mines? In her long years of wandering through cities and towns carrying out missions for the underground, she had switched vocations dozens of times. But she had never done work like this.

We sat next to each other, a German newspaper in my hands, which I translated word by word. "The patch must be round, of the color yellow; it must be ten centimeters in diameter. It must be placed on the right side of the chest and on the shoulder, at exactly the same height...."

From Myetek's military rucksack, which during our long four-hundred-kilometer march on foot had turned the color of faded harvest grass, Marilya cut off a clean bit of canvas and set about preparing my "entrance permit" to the ghetto.

Marilya was convinced that my decision to go into the ghetto meant pretty much the same thing we had done during the years of the underground: infiltrating an environment where we had to "look the part," to carry out an assignment for the Party. So as not to leave any doubt in my mind, she recounted:

"One time, with my goyish [she really said that!] appearance—I ended up in a Jewish town. The householders could not be permitted the slightest suspicion that I was not Jewish. I'd learned a few Yiddish words in prison, but to put them all together in a sentence was beyond me. And as it happened, my small-town landlord was always hanging around me, trying to draw me into a conversation. I went this way, that way—I couldn't get away from him. Suddenly a whole phrase popped into my mouth that always made our Jewish girls in prison laugh: "You have as much sense as the Chelmer chazn's turkey!" So, like a fool, I blurt out this adage ... and guess what? The business could have been a disaster for me: it turned out that my landlord actually was from Chelm ...."

Our laughter left Myetshislav Kozak utterly indifferent. While Marilya began sewing the patches to my garment, he only grumbled for the umpteenth time his "To hell with this whole game," and once more lapsed into frozen silence.

Truth be told, I myself hadn't taken this business of going off to the ghetto as something calamitous. Only now did Marilya's last words unsettle me:

"Here you go, you're all ready. Dressed up just like you were paying a visit to Red Cross Street...."

All told, how many years had it been? It was on just such a hot summer day, in a secret apartment in Warsaw, that I was helped to dress up to look as much as possible "high-society ready."

I had a meeting in a very aristocratic house on Red Cross Street, the home of a high ministerial official of the government then in power.

This memory began to press upon my heart, till my throat grew tight, and before my eyes loomed up the still-unbuilt ghetto wall that would soon separate me from my two battle comrades.

It was actually Myetshislav who, at the last moment of our parting, diffused my dark thoughts by reminding me that it was not just today that we had chosen this path on which every step was accompanied by dangers.

We hugged each other, kissed, and in my ear I heard the whispered saying that always accompanied us on perilous paths:

"Stay strong, old man!"

"Stay strong, old man!" ... With that, I had been seen off some ten years earlier, on a mission to the great Bialovezsh forest.

That was a year of immense social upheaval in Poland. Along with the Lodz and Bialystok textile workers, thousands of peasants from entire districts had joined the fight. From village to village, the call went forth: Resist! From the Bialystok province the struggle spread to the regions of Slonim, Pinsk, and Baranovitsh. Peasant lumberjacks and log drivers took up their weapons to stand against the punitive expeditions of the police. The headquarters of the movement was located in the enormous Bialovezsh forest. It was to assist this very headquarters staff that I had been sent.

It was difficult to crawl through the closely set police outposts that were attempting to lay siege to the rebels. But it was immeasurably harder to approach the fighters' headquarters. Here there was forest, and here were patrols with weapons in their hands. Woe to any stranger who meant to sneak through to the center of the fighting camp!

This was the introductory school to our later partisan fight.

There would be other schools.

September 1939. The Hitlerist assault on Poland has already lasted fourteen days and we, five hundred prisoners of the Polish Sanacja regime, still sit locked up in the narrow cells of the Brisk prison. The tapping from cell to cell has become more agitated. When the "conversation" with Teodor Kovalevski is finished, the "telegraph" goes out to Yuzef Kofman, after that to the Ukrainian Tatsi, to White Russian Juk, and soon comes the general rallying cry:

"Break down the doors!"

We are already in the prison courtyard. The Hitlerists are twenty kilometers from us, yet there is no sign of panic here whatsoever. Everyone waits for our command.

We set out for the nearest village. Decisions must be made on the fly. We will consult with those in whose name we are fighting—with the people. What next?

TO THE WOODS! TO THE PARTISAN STRUGGLE!

* *
*

This test of our battle-readiness lasted for a total of three days. But it was these three days that gave us the chance to identify secure forest trails and paths. And above all, to recognize the courageous nature of those who, two years later in the days of the people's greatest despair, during the Hitler assault, straight away proclaimed the watchword of struggle and liberation:

TO THE WOODS! TO THE PARTISAN STRUGGLE!

They, the "Jews without yellow stars," were among the first to lead thousands of ordinary people into the woods, with weapons in their hands and the oath of the fallen Jewish warrior-poet Osher Schwartzman on their lips:

I will not return unto this land
Until the word of full redemption is at hand.

Warsaw, 1947.

Historical Notes: *Smolar describes the initial story scene as taking place outside the ghetto, as the three of them are sitting on the "still intact little bridge at the old Writers House" (TMG, 13). Smolar names them in Polish as Mieczslaw Kozak and Marila Dziekan and says that Kozak was a Polish union leader and Dziekan a coal regions trade union leader (TMG, 9). He writes: "She and Kozak were my 'cover'—traveling with them I was not a Jew."*

Smolar mentions Myetshislav Kozak in both his 1975 memoir Vu Bistu Khaver Sidorov? *(166) and* Fun Minsker Geto *(98), describing Myetshislav Kozak as a Polish comrade who "died a hero's death in the partisan struggle."*

The "Red Cross Street" in Warsaw that Smolar mentions, in Polish "Czerwonego Krzyża," is located in the Powiśle district of the city. It gets its name from a small Red Cross hospital built on it. A section of the Warsaw Ghetto, it was later part of the site of the Ghetto Uprising.

The textile workers' strike that Smolar refers to was likely a large strike that went from 6 March 1933 to 5 April 1933. Strikers included those from

Łódź, Żyrardów, and Białystok, and six people died in the struggle. This strike was the largest industrial event occurring in Poland during the interwar years (Hiemstra-Kuperus 2016, 411).

The Yiddish poet Osher (Asher) Schwartzman (1890-1919), "the first Soviet Yiddish poet to fall in battle for the Soviet Union, in 1919, became the challenging model for Soviet Yiddish writers: to follow Asher with pen and rifle, whenever land and people would stand exposed to danger" (American 1985, 80).

Foreword to the 1952 Edition

The first edition of Hersh Smolar's book "Jews without Yellow Stars" has sold out completely. The publisher "Yidish Bukh" continues to receive hundreds of letters from this country and abroad requesting this book.

This is a good sign. It signifies that Jewish people do not want to forget what took place, and that especially now, considering the grave dangers which lie in wait for us today—the perils of a new world war—they want to understand those ordinary but heroic borderless "Jews without Yellow Stars," of whom the book's author tells. The Jewish masses around the world are determined not to permit the brown beast, shaped by the Anglo-Saxon weapons manufacturers, to threaten once again the lives of millions, above all the lives of Jews. The example of the partisans, of the ghetto resistance fighters, strengthens the courage and the will of the Jewish masses to resist with all their might the bearers of new, even more terrible calamities.

And just as the "Jews without Yellow Stars," arrayed in battle with all people who detested the fascist war-eradicators, fought for their lives, so the ordinary, honest Jewish people today stand in one row with all those who fight for peace worldwide.

For these Jews, the publisher "Yidish Bukh" presents the second edition of Hersh Smolar's "Jews without Yellow Stars." This version is an improved one, and the author has added to it a sequence of narratives that were written in the heat of the moment, with rifle in hand.

Publisher "Yidish Bukh"
by the Social-Cultural Association of the Jews in Poland

Warsaw, 1952.

Historical Notes: "The Jewish Social-Cultural Association in Poland (*Towarzystwo Społeczno-Kulturalne Żydów w Polsce; TSKŻ*) was established in 1950 as a government-sanctioned secular organization in place of previous Jewish organizations that were somewhat autonomous. As relics of the People's Republic, TSKŻs still exist today in some cities in Poland (as independent organizations now) but are mostly dying. Religious congregations took over and other secular organizations were established."

—*Courtesy of Piotr Nazuruk*
 Grodzka Gate–NN Theatre Centre
 Lublin, Poland

A Good Morning!

How long they had been sitting that way, contorted, crushed together, no one knew. In the hiding place beneath the cobblestoned Jewish Cemetery Lane, there sounded the deafening beat of continuous gunfire, the hasty running of heavy hobnailed boots. But not a single ray of light reached in. By day it was as pitch-black as by night. In the first hours—who knows, maybe entire days?—one tried, with strained, squinting eyes, to pierce the absolute darkness, to seek a sign of light.

Later, the eyelids began to droop down heavily on their own. At that very moment, it seemed that it was beginning to grow bright. The more firmly the eyelids pressed together, the brighter it became—so bright that at times a golden, sunny beam would dazzle the eyes and leave a refreshing warmth.

But all this was later. Much later (who knows how many hours or days?). At first, without conferring, everyone tried to hold their breath, to choke it back inside. If anyone drew in a loud breath, a hiss like a snake's was immediately heard from all sides, and the person could actually sense a murderous fury ready to tear him to pieces. Everyone's ears were pricked, not to miss the slightest rustle from above. And once, at precisely such a moment, a child burst out crying.

A pit full of people swayed. In the crush of bodies, a space suddenly opened. Hands began tearing their way towards the corner from where the child's wails carried.

"Strangle it!"

A woman's cut-off, muted spasm beat back the swaying human knot. And once again it became cramped in the pit, even more cramped than before. The undischarged malice was released in a rasping breath; for some, even in a wheezing screech. Beads of cold sweat rolled down from the forehead into the eyes, to the nose, where they remained as if solidified.

A round from an automatic rifle carried over the pit. Soon after, a second, a third, a fourth . . . .

As it became quiet once again, no trace of the tension remained in the pit. People began trying to straighten their backs, to stretch out a hand, to wet their parched lips with their tongues.

"How late can it be now?"

No one answered. But no one was annoyed by the question either. Rather, many were curious to know whether it was night out in the world, or day. The few human words, heard for the first time in the muted pit, sent forth a breath of life. The reverberations of gunfire and heavy soldier-steps broke through the intermittent calm. That meant the "Aktion" was continuing. But there was no longer any fear. There was only fatigue, which overflowed into their minds and limbs as if a tightly coiled spring had been removed. People began to breathe deeply.

A child started crying, first with a muffled whimper that quickly became louder, clearer. Suddenly the wailing was interrupted. In the exhausted silence was heard the smacking of childish lips that had received the mother's breast.

"Well, look who's awake. A good morning to you, child of mine . . . ."

The people in the pit distinctly felt as if a fresh morning breeze were blowing through the dense darkness.

Historical Notes: *"Malinas," such as the one these people are hiding in, were common in most ghettos. According to Smolar (TMG 1989, 27), the word comes from criminal vocabulary, and was used for the various hideouts and bunkers constructed in every conceivable place in the ghettos. They ranged in size from a space that barely one person could squeeze into, to spaces that could accommodate several hundred (72). The Minsk Judenrat had a malina big enough for several hundred people constructed under the ghetto workshops, with a tunnel dug under the fence to facilitate escape from the ghetto (Epstein 2008, 139). Smolar himself spent weeks in* *a malina behind a false wall, a crawl space so narrow that he could only stand up or lie on his side* (TMG 1989, 94). After Minsk was liberated, a man named Bubler recounted that "he had been among seventeen Jews who, before the ghetto was annihilated, constructed an underground chamber in the Jewish cemetery. They disguised its entry and exit with planks, and they inserted tin pipes that allowed some air in, but not enough; many in the hiding place died of lack of air" (Epstein 2008, 108).

Smolar also describes a malina constructed in the ghetto just prior to the 2 March 1942 massacre of 5,000 ghetto Jews: "A 'malina' to accommodate several hundred men was prepared in the workshops of the Board, with an exit into the city" (RM 1966, 43).

T'khies Hameysim
(Resurrection of the Dead)

Not so much out of fear, but because of Etl's cry, "The bandits are coming!" the residents in the packed room, trembling, remained standing in utter impotence. By the time they recovered their wits and rushed to hide whatever they could lay hands on, the door was already flung open. A swarm of Jewish ghetto police fanned out across the room, searching, rummaging, shaking things.

"Give it up yourself. You'll be better off."

Before anyone could find out what sorts of items they must give up voluntarily—that it was a matter of a new edict demanding fur garments for the Germans—pieces of soap, chunks of salt, shoes were already flying into the ghetto policemen's sacks....

It was then that they came across Efron.

Exactly when he had settled himself into the room, no one knew. Surely, they surmised, after the second Nazi Aktion when, in the increasingly cramped ghetto rooms, people began "building" second and third floors—"reserved spaces." People hung ropes along the walls, laid boards on them, and these became at first places to lie down, and later corners for entire families.

One of the policemen made his way to the "third floor" looking for hiding places. Suddenly he let loose a mouthful of curses, that men were being hidden there... that they don't go to work... snoozing in broad daylight... and endangering a ghetto full of Jews.

The people stand there, not knowing what to say. The policeman lets loose a series of blows onto a body, so resoundingly that it could be heard below. He makes a quick descent, stammering something, until the circle of frightened women and children find out that "It's just a corpse. It already stinks."

After the gang of Jewish police left the room, the first one to climb up to the "third floor" was ten-year-old Natek.

"Oh no, it's the teacher!" he shouted down from above.

Several boys went up after him, and slowly began to lower the seemingly lifeless male body. Someone felt his pulse and detected a weak sign of life. Women began to bustle around him. They poured water on him, massaged his temples, and for a second the man opened one eye. A quiet groan escaped his tightly clenched teeth, and then once again he lay limp.

It evolved on its own, the custom in the room, that when a family would cook a bit of dinner, they would call Natek to take a few spoonfuls to "the corpse," meaning Efron.

* *
*

After those two days in which, along with a third of the Jews, Efron's wife and both children were taken away, it could have happened in any ghetto room: someone came in and no one asked him what he wanted, why he had settled just there. Everyone was so submerged in his own suffering that generally nobody noticed anybody else. And so Efron, unnoticed, had crawled into a corner, onto a heap of old clothes, and there he lay. Later he moved up above. Someone had pointed out an open spot to him, and this same "someone" had given Efron a shove from below, literally heaved him up to the third floor.

It was only after they had resuscitated him that what had happened to him began to sink in. He had completely lost his ability to cope with it. If he strained, if he tried to recall something, his head would become heavy as a stone, and his eyes would close with fatigue, unable to be kept open.

Sitting there next to him is little Natek, looking at him with warm compassionate eyes—that he, Efron, should at least answer him with a smile, stretch out a hand to give a caress. Nothing! Even the bit of warm soup that Natek pours down his throat, he, Efron, makes not the slightest effort to swallow.

"Eat, teacher, and you will get well."

Actually, he isn't at all sick, there's no pain in any of his limbs, but when he wants to tell this to Natek, he can't bring any sound out of his throat.

"Teacher," he calls him. Why on earth does he call him teacher?

The furrows on Efron's forehead swell, his eyes open wide and sharply scrutinize Natek's face. From the great exertion, beads of sweat accumulate in the deep brow-wrinkle and run down straight into his eyes. Efron feels as if very thin spears were stabbing him in the pupils. Tears begin to stream out without ceasing.

"Eat, teacher, and you will get well," repeats Natek, as he moves the little pot of warm food up to Efron. And because Natek's eyes are also flowing with tears, he doesn't notice how Efron suddenly attacks the food greedily.

The loud smacking of Efron's lips after each swallow, accompanied by a weird snorting from his swollen nostrils, at first gave Natek a fright. He even attempted to lower one foot down from the bunk, but suddenly felt upon him Efron's gaze, in which lay the former authority that would calm a rowdy classroom and force them to listen attentively as he examined them: What happens next?

As it used to happen in the classroom when the teacher was dissatisfied with an inadequately answered question, a heaviness began to press on Natek's mind as he sought something that would compel Efron, the teacher, to pronounce his restrained satisfied "Enough, sit down." But before he managed to come up with something, he was met with the teacher's verdict:

"Nothing. It's hopeless. Finished."

Suddenly Natek remembered something that once, during an exam, he had heard the teacher himself say:

"It's finished, so we must begin again."

Natek completely forgot that he had before him the once-strict teacher, Efron. He became stubborn in his insistence: It is not hopeless—one must, one can, one should . . . .

"What?"

Natek bent down closer to Efron and began murmuring in his ear, as if it were a secret, about those people who are going away, about those who are preparing themselves, who are doing....

Efron was prepared to disdainfully dismiss these boyish dreams born of desperation. But close to his ear he heard the quiet, secretive whispering:

"We too, from your school, have decided...."

For an instant there flashed before Efron's eyes the white light of the classroom, and the dozens of intensely eager eyes of his students who listened intently to his words. Out of old habit, he passed his hand over his balding head—a sign that he had yet to introduce his main ideas.

"When you gather together, let me know."

Historical Notes: *The second Aktion mentioned in the story may be the one conducted on 20 November 1941, from Zamkovaya Street to the east edge of the ghetto. During this "pogrom" (the Soviet word for Aktion), between 5,000 and 10,000 Jews were murdered at the Tutshinka execution site (Epstein 2008, 101).*

Like other large ghettos, the Minsk ghetto was extremely overcrowded, holding at its height over 100,000 people (Epstein, 42). Some apartments held between 20 and 30 people, and it was not uncommon for bunk beds ("floors" in the story) to be constructed (Epstein, 86). The overcrowding was compounded by people fearing to leave their apartments because of the constant roundups and violence on the streets (Epstein, 89).

Smolar uses the term "militia-men" to refer to the ghetto Jewish Police Service, rather than the more commonly used terms Ordnungsdienst ("Order Service") or Jewish ghetto police. When Ilya Mushkin, the first head of the Minsk Judenrat, set up its administrative structure, he copied the internal designs of Soviet bureaucracies, including the naming of departments such as "militsiia" for law enforcement (Finkel 2017, 76). The brutality of the Jewish ghetto police and their collaboration with the German authorities is a well-known and highly controversial topic. Smolar describes the hatred felt toward them by Minsk ghetto residents as they would confiscate their property—sometimes by decree to fulfill a Nazi demand for specific items or ransom, sometimes for their own enrichment: "The Jewish police went from house to house conducting thorough searches in which they often uncovered hiding places and confiscated everything that people had been keeping to exchange for food. In some cases, the searchers took things that were not even 'on the list'" (TMG 1989, 53-54).

Emanuel Ringelblum, chronicler of the Warsaw Ghetto archives, famously noted that the cruelty of the ghetto police was "at times greater than that of the Germans, the Ukrainians and the Latvians" (Gutman 1994, 143). Yet the first leaders of the Minsk ghetto focused on cooperation with the Germans for the good of the community, rather than collaboration. Both Ilya Mushkin and Ziama Serebrianskii, the first commander of Minsk's Jewish police, were active in the Minsk underground. Both were eventually arrested: Mushkin in February 1942, who simply vanished; Serebrianskii was publicly hanged in May along with 27 other underground members (Epstein 2008, 135). After this, the Jewish ghetto police increasingly consisted of Polish ghetto Jews, who had little connection with the residents (Finkel 2017, 78).

The Jewish police were given better rations, better quarters; starvation and deportation were perhaps temporarily avoided. Ultimately, however, the status of the Jewish police spared neither them nor their families.

There were Jewish police who refused to carry out the Germans' orders, and those who committed suicide rather than continue on. When rounding up the ghetto Jews for deportation—including their own families—Perechodnik speaks with admiration of fellow Otwock ghetto policeman Abram Willendorf's actions: "He says nothing to his wife; silently removes and throws aside his armband, hat, and number; and calmly sits on the ground. We are going away together, such is the silent answer of Willendorf, an honorable man" (Perechodinik 1996, 39).

Under the Ground

The signal was this: a young lad would be cleaning the cobblestone pavement at the corner of Cemetery Way, and the lining of his coat would be turned with the fur facing out. He should be asked: "Where do you take out the garbage from the ghetto?" He'll then show the way....

As Sasha's order and the pass-phrase was being conveyed to him, Shloyme Nisn assumed a face of indifference, as if to say, "We are already well versed in these tricks of the underground." But internally his heart gave an extra-strong beat. Something was up. Surely it was the eve of an Aktion. And although he was exhausted from a day of hard slave labor building the German garage, and hungry to the point where his intestines were twisted up inside him, he couldn't seem to find a spot to sit down for a little rest and get a bite to eat. However, so that none of his neighbors should notice his agitation, he began rummaging among the few personal belongings that lay in the corner by his sleeping place. Apparently his neighbor Dvoyre (people called her "his ghetto-wife") did indeed notice his turmoil. She asked him where he was getting ready to go at such a late hour. He wanted to cover himself—in case he was gone the entire night—and therefore, quietly, with feigned nonchalance, told her a story about an opportunity:

"It might be that I'll be grinding away all night to earn some money... a hideout for someone."

He noticed the boy from a distance, immediately recognizing that he was very jittery: Instead of sweeping the pavement, the lad kept turning around in one spot with the "torch" in his hand. He, Shloyme Nisn, had not even managed to finish reciting the pass-phrase when the boy laid everything out crisp and clear to him and added, in a reproachful voice, "When one says six o'clock—it should be six."

In the morgue he was met by Sasha, who said, "I thought you were no longer around," and angrily ordered Shloyme Nisn to follow him.

From Sasha's steely and confident gaze, Shloyme Nisn gathered that no misfortune had occurred. What was happening here was probably a necessary bit of work. And only then did he feel as if the fatigue of the difficult day had settled in his legs, which began to stumble as he climbed deeper into the cellar beneath the morgue.

Even before Sasha said it, Shloyme Nisn clearly sensed that there were others there. But the darkness was so dense that he could not even detect Sasha near him.

"Briefly said: From this day forward you are dead, and you received your burial here, on a floor lower than the actual dead."

Sasha was quiet for a minute, as if he were waiting to see what kind of impression his strange words made on those assembled.

Sasha's words rang so strangely that no one raised a single question.

"None of you has any family, so there will be none to mourn you, unless... perhaps someone has left behind a ghetto-wife" (Shloyme Nisn felt the jab—"He knows everything, this secret policeman"), "but this doesn't count. So, they will now be ghetto-widows."

Someone let out a giggle. Someone else, feeling cheered up, tried to respond with a word. A small electric lantern lit up in Sasha's hand, and with squinting eyes everyone bent forward, curiously looking at each other.

Besides Sasha, there were five or six more men and one woman.

"You'll have time to get acquainted," Sasha spoke, once again in darkness. And although his voice now sounded harsher, the words became sparser. And as do members of a military squad, each person began to feel more at home, self-confident.

The matter became clearer. No one would return to the ghetto; either death here on the spot, or... that, they would discover later. For that, each one would receive a guarantee as a last resort: a small dose of poison. The task was an urgent one, and it was only to them—who had already proved themselves—that the matter was entrusted. A tunnel must be dug. The direction, the length, the deadline—all this Sonya knew. She was the leader; she was responsible. Communications, food, news—these they would receive through Finkel (the one with the broom). Now was not the time to describe it more precisely—this, the engineer, Sonya, would do. One thing they must know: it was a task of great signific ance.

"The issue is this: that there, where death reigns, life should blossom forth, and such life!... Understood? Well, you'll catch on later. Now—" and again the lantern blazed in Sasha's hand, "now, back to work."

He exchanged kisses with each one of them, and when they had digested it all, they heard only the trickling of sand after lowering the cellar cover.

* *
*

Everyone waited to hear a word from Sonya, but she could find no suitable words to continue Sasha's command-speech. The silence became overwhelming for everyone. Something must be done, after all, and quickly at that. Someone began shuffling his feet, and soon lowered himself to the ground. After him, the rest of them. Sonya bit her lip, not knowing what to say in this situation to remind the group that she was the one in charge. She felt that it was foolish, that it was after the fact, but nevertheless she said, "Sit down for a bit. Rest up. Soon we'll go into action."

Later Sonya recalled that it was Shloyme Nisn who, as if with a wave of his hand, removed the sense of alienation, and they began to feel bound together with one secret, one goal, one destiny.

"Twenty years in a row I've been in the underground. Where haven't I been! What kind of work haven't I done already! However, under the ground, there I've never been before. It's always been puzzling to me: why do they call it the 'underground'? More often than not, we were up in attics... So Hitler had to come along and demonstrate it to me."

"Twenty years, you say?" a squeaky man's voice responded. "And I, an hour after coming into the movement, felt as if I lived on two floors at the same time. Oh, what troubles did I have to endure, when the addresses would sometimes get mixed up in my mind. At least now it's clear—one address..."

"At the cemetery," someone muttered under their breath.

"Apparently you didn't know everything," a gruff voice interjected, and quickly broke off. Instead of words, a quiet giggling could be heard from that spot.

"And what did you know?" whispered Shloyme Nisn, with resentment that it had to be dragged out of the other speaker. "A secret perhaps? A conspiracy!"

The response was the same giggling, but now it resembled more a stifled coughing in the chest.

"Oh, yes. And what a conspiracy! How many years have gone by, and nobody hears anything about this? What do you know about young people who glimpsed not a ray of light for months, who gagged on their own blood every time their lungs tried to take a deeper breath? How many times did I urge them, 'Go up above, the Party will let you take a rest, get well...' No one went. They knew: They'd never make it back underground."

"You worked in a print shop?" said Sonya with a start. The rest of them thought her surprise came from being the first to realize about the kind of group he was telling them about.

Soon, however, there penetrated into everyone's ears the soft whisper of a woman's voice, secretively unveiling the great thing with which they had been entrusted: From the depths of this very earth shall come forth the true word. Those who believe not, will acquire faith; those who have despaired, will be heartened; those who wait, will hearken to the command; those who stand in battle, will double their blows.

"There will be a print shop here?"

"With an exit on both sides of the world—not just on this side, but also on 'the other side'..."

Someone lit a match; another provided a candle. No one sought the other's face. They got up from their places, sought out the chisels that lay ready for them, and in the meantime, Sonya was already standing before them and wordlessly drawing with a shovel the length and breadth of the tunnel.

Historical Notes: *After entering the Minsk ghetto, Smolar soon encountered other communist cadres he knew and trusted. Under his leadership, an underground organization was formed (Finkel 2017, 165). The first meeting was 17 August 1941. One of the members was Notke Wainhoyz, a colleague of Smolar's and former editor of a well-known children's newspaper in Minsk (Epstein 2008, 117). It was too dangerous for Wainhoyz to leave his hiding place in the ghetto, so Smolar presented his recommendation: "He proposed one single task: to combat the illusions of the Jews in the ghetto about 'waiting out' the war, protecting themselves in 'good work places.' This would be done by word of mouth and by written propaganda" (TMG 1989, 29).*

Smolar later connected with Nokhem Feldman's group, among whose members were several printers who were smuggling fonts out of Proryv Printing House, a former newspaper publishing house now under German control, where they worked. This group formed a ghetto underground press that printed leaflets, reported on the Red Army resistance to the German army, and also a "newspaper" called "News from the Motherland" (Epstein 2008, 156). After the arrests (and murder) of multiple members in September 1942, the press was shut down, the fonts were hidden, and the remaining members fled to the forest (Epstein, 162).

At the same time as the formation of the press, Smolar, together with Feldman's group, set up an underground workshop in a cellar on Ostrovski Street. Headed by Misha Tshiptshin, they printed false documents, leaflets, and news bulletins from the front (TMG 1989, 34).

Certainty

Those who knew Sholem Ayngorn from before the first pogrom would even now, encountering his column on their return from work in the ghetto, try to determine through hints whether anything important had taken place. That Sholem would bring news—of this there was no doubt. Such an expert as was he in collecting information, there was none second to him in the ghetto. From an unfinished word from the Herr Chief while drawing him into a conversation, from a line read in the "Shock Troop" or "Eagle in the East," even from the expression on the colonel's face during his daily visit to the workshops where Jews and prisoners of war worked—from all these things, Sholem managed to extract news.

In the evening, when a dead silence reigned over the ghetto, when gates were tightly shut under lock and key, the neighbors would gather at Sholem's place and he, calmly, in the voice of a radio announcer, would deliver the latest news. And all these news items were uplifting, truly redemptive. Jews would leave Sholem's with a light step, lost in dreams about the longed-for day that was already near, the day that was just around the corner and would bring an end to all the troubles.

What came, however, were autumn days, very difficult ones. While gathering together at Sholem's place, someone would now let out a sigh; someone else would even let fall a bitter word:

"Troubles like stacks of wood, but no fuel to heat with . . . ."

Nevertheless, not a single day was allowed to pass without a visit to Sholem. To get the daily allotment of news had become an organic need. Without this, there could be no question of ending the uneasy ghetto day.

After the first pogrom, all this came to an end. Very few of the original neighbors remained alive. Whoever did manage to escape with their lives went and buried themselves straight after work in their own corners. And above all, even Sholem Ayngorn no longer knew anything, as if all the sources of information had suddenly dried up.

Old Hurvitsh would still sometimes come in to see him (the one of whom it was said that he made a living from Sholem's news: he went around from house to house, read from a scrap of paper what "the radio says," and for that received a bowl of soup, a piece of bread). He used to sit, the old man, gaze into Sholem's frozen stare, and with a quiet groan take himself away to his sleeping corner.

During work in the Germans' tailor-workshop, people would now speak but little. If someone did interject a word, it would barely reach Sholem's ears.

Sholem lost his certainty, that certainty that used to rise up in him after he, with his news, had animated those insubstantial souls who were half-extinguished by despair. Often now, he would jerk away from his machine at the slightest creak and remain standing all atremble. At night he would climb down from his sleeping place, stand for a long time at the window, and stare at the fence, which did not admit even the smallest sliver of sky.

Later on, it began to seem to Sholem that he was regaining his lost certainty. He had noticed that when arranging themselves in formation to go back to the ghetto, in the tailor shop cutter Gelbart's group of four there were always three workers who during the walk would cleverly exchange words in such a way that no one else could hear. Sholem began to seek access to Gelbart, tried to renew his well of knowledge of current events, to draw him into a conversation, and to extract what Gelbart guarded from everyone around him. Sholem was just about certain he had made it to the inner circle. A job had even been entrusted to him: smuggling out from the workshop whatever he could; it was required. Sholem understood who required it. He himself, Sholem, required it—that sense of certainty. After all, he himself belonged to those who would not allow themselves to be slaughtered.

Little by little, Sholem's anxiety ebbed away. His silence now possessed the depth of a closely guarded secret. Now his ears would no longer pick up peripheral conversations—they interfered with his spinning the dream that he, Sholem, was bringing closer the day of redemption. But he did talk all day long, often in the middle of the night—with himself.

It was on that early morning when the Judenrat agent told the German escort for the column of tailors that he could lead them off to the worksite—"No one else is coming"—that the armor protecting Sholem's painfully acquired certainty suddenly shattered. Other workers tried pulling him by the sleeve, to draw him off; Sholem pushed them all away. He walked up to the Judenrat agent in alarm: "What do you mean, no one else is coming? So, and the cutter? And the rest of the tailors, where are they?"

The ghetto police drove him back into line, and although it was clear to everyone from the policemen's speech—"Maybe you'd like to go there too? It's a very secure place!"—that there was nothing more to ask, Sholem kept repeating the entire way his "What do you mean? Where are they?" What a worker had told him never seemed to penetrate his awareness: "The Gestapo were searching the ghetto all night, looking for partisans." The question mark remained on his face.

Just before the end of the workday, Sholem suddenly got up from his machine and began bustling about the workshop. The warnings from the other workers that the chief might come at any moment had no effect. Sholem went to the cutting table, and rummaging around, sought out and stealthily began to stash in his breast pocket the large cutting scissors. A worker noticed this and calmly, as if in jest, asked Sholem:

"Planning to do some sewing in the ghetto? To cut out something?"

Sholem's eyes tensely focused on him and loudly, as if with a voice not his own, he declared:

"Yes, I'll cut, I'll be doing some cutting; what else would I be doing?"

It would sometimes happen that at night Sholem would awake with a start from his restless ghetto-sleep, touch the place where the scissors lay, and drained from the great effort, fall back down on his sleeping place.

Historical Notes: *Actual news reports were a scarcity in the ghettos, with outside newspapers and radios forbidden. Jews were especially desperate for some type of good news to help them cope with their horrific situation (Finkel 2017, 55). In his book* The Minsk Ghetto *(25), Smolar discusses these reports, which were known as "news from YIVO—(Yidn Viln Azoy—Jews want it this way)." He describes how they "acted as a narcotic that helped people hold out against the incessant German roundups in the ghetto streets and during the terrible nights behind the barricaded doors of their houses." He describes how "the ghetto even saw the birth of a new profession of news broadcasters," including one who, like Old Hurvitsh in this story, at "every house into which he brought his good news from the fronts, he was given a 'meal.'"*

Finkel notes that "[A] 'news agency' with the very same name (YIVO) is also mentioned in the Bialystok ghetto, even though we lack any evidence of communication between the two ghettos" (Finkel 2017, 56).

At the Edge

The more furiously the snowstorm raged, the calmer at heart Iser became. He was in such good spirits that he forgot his own command—"Lie like the dead! Don't move a muscle!"—and began rubbing his hands together, massaging his shoulders, in order to generate a little warmth.

The wind tore at the last shingles of the ruined house that stood at the edge of the ghetto. The snow spun wildly in the void, till it collapsed exhausted onto the heaps of garbage that had been tossed there. Dressed in white robes made of sheets, each person in the group that Iser was supposed to lead out of the ghetto that day looked like a mound of snow. No one budged from his spot. Iser began to feel sorry for his comrades, so he began clambering over to one and then another:

"What do you say, eh? Drops of gold are falling! Everything is going to go well—extra smoothly, by special order!"

He grasped at once that his example could stir up the group, and quickly settled himself down, straining his ears to catch what was going on, there on the outside.

The angry wind harassed first one wall of the ruined house and then another wall; unable to overcome them, it made its way through the holes in the roof, through any crevice available, penetrating the bones of the concealed Jews.

At times it seemed to Iser that the snowstorm was abating. Then he would quickly draw his head out from the warmth of his chest and at once realize that in fact he had begun to doze off. He became uneasy. He might even fail to hear the signal from the other side. That was the last thing he needed. In such a case he would pay with his own head. Iser sharpened his hearing even more, though he knew it was not yet time, that the rooster's crow—the sign from the "other side"—could only come after the changing of the police guard at the edge of the ghetto. Not trusting himself, Iser bent down to the nearest "mound" and murmured to him that he should pass along the message: "Don't allow the person next to you to doze off, everyone should listen hard, because any minute now...."

There could be no doubt: downhill from the city, in the direction of the ghetto, a truck was approaching. For a moment, the wind carried to the ruined house the distant noise of not one, but several motors.

"Stay still!" Iser roared, although no one had stirred from their spot.

He furtively approached the outside door, laid his ear to it, and on tiptoe laboriously found a crack.

"They must be driving by on their way to the highway," he announced, bending down, and again stood still, trying with a squinting eye to glimpse some sign of the trucks, which should already have been close by. But aside from the dreary circle dance of the wind and snow, he saw nothing. He could hear that it fell silent around them, as if the trucks had been ripped out of the landscape. Iser lowered himself back to the ground, but his mood of certainty that everything would go off in good order had evaporated. If it had gone quiet, this was a sign that the trucks had stopped in the ghetto. Now, in the middle of the night—that meant....

He had not managed to bring to mind the series of pogroms of some time ago, which had ripped away pieces of the ghetto night after night, when upon the ruined house descended a flood of light-daggers that penetrated every hole. Everyone lurched from their places: some crept deep into corners, others in blind haste made a dash towards the exit. From someone there burst out a startled "Oh!"

"Hit the dirt!" Iser bellowed, in a manner that froze everyone in their tracks. And so they remained, until the light turned away from the house and lit up a side section of the ghetto.

"Heroes, already with full underpants...."

No one was insulted by Iser's ridicule. Indeed it was so: they were terrified. A little thing—here someone suddenly grabs you by the throat, and you are supposed to lie there and not move an inch. *Yes, but nevertheless, now we have weapons, any minute now and we'll cross the boundary of the ghetto and then . . .* They were surely heading towards a life of ceaseless pursuit by the enemy's spotlights, bullets, airplanes, spies, and traitors. *Yes, but this will be on the other side . . . here we are still in the ghetto . . . .*

But when from the other end of the ghetto came a wild bellowing from the SS troops intermingled with the crying and shrieking of the women and children, when one series of machine gun fire after another drowned out the howling of the wind and the voices of the tormented—no one in the ruined house made any further unnecessary movements. Everyone had their eyes fixed on Iser's face, awaiting his order, which surely must come soon. And the order did come:

"Partisans, hear my command! Weapons—to the ready! . . . ."

The Last Letters

"Wait a minute!"

It was already high time to leave! Each minute truly threatened catastrophe—they had to get to the assembly place where the columns of workers were gathered, while it was still full of people. In the commotion they would not be conspicuous, the group of five armed men who must soon leave the ghetto forever. But Reuben had stopped everyone so suddenly with his impulsive "Wait a minute!" that the rest of them stood there bewildered. No one had time to even ask, "What for?"—when Reuben ripped the photograph of his little six-year-old daughter from the wall and quickly began to write on its left side:

> "I bid you farewell, my one and only. We will never see each other again....
>
> "It's been exactly three months since they took you away from me and killed you. When the murderers took your mother away from us both, you were all that remained to me. And afterwards—alone, all alone... what is there to live for?
>
> "I say goodbye to you now, my little daughter, and I say to you: I want to live, I want very, very much to live! I want my hands to feel the taste of vengeance for your mother, for you, my only one, for our good and beloved friends, of which you and I and all of us had so many. I take my leave of you, dear daughter of mine.
>
> "Your papa"

Reuben closed his eyes for a minute, as if willing himself to recall something, and soon began hastily scribbling again.

"To Herr Oberleutnant Shermark

"Don't look for me, Herr Oberleutnant. You considered me a 'decent Jude.' I quietly bore the heavy yoke of a ghetto Jew. I toiled for you, received as payment your constant curses, insults, and often blows. Be advised, Oberleutnant Shermark: Reuben Heiblum, the Jude from the ghetto, is no more! Now there is the partisan, the vengeance-taker, who will pay you back for each spilled drop of innocent blood—I'll pay you back many times over . . . and should you insist on searching for me—please do: I'll be in all the surrounding woods. I've exchanged my carpenter's saw and plane for a rifle, the rifle that I took from you. And if you want nonetheless to meet me—please do."

When Reuben was out in the street, the last worker group moved out.

Historical Notes: *A few details about Reuben Heiblum (Haibloom) are given by the Organization of Partisans, Underground Fighters and Ghetto Rebels in Israel. Reuben was a Polish Jew who knew German, and was used as forced labor by the Germans to handle military communications equipment. He was able to uncover some German army plans, including locations of mines in Minsk and other places. As in the story, he stole a weapon from the Germans, fled to the forest, and joined the partisans. As part of the Lazo Regiment, he was killed in battle in the Naliboki forest.*

Much of the same information is also found in Smolar's other texts. Smolar describes a mission (TMG 1989, 80): "Heading this group was Reuben Haibloom, a Jewish worker from Poland. After his only daughter was murdered during the Purim pogrom [Minsk ghetto 2 March 1942] he volunteered for the most dangerous sabotage missions."

Shlomo Strauss-Marko describes Smolar setting off on a mission with a group of four partisans, one of them being Reuben Heiblum (Strauss-Marko 1983, 96-97).

A Night in the Forest

Certainly it was not from fatigue that everyone's feet began to stumble terribly. With every damp leaf that fell on someone's face, on their bowed neck, or on their clothes, the sweat-soaked body reacted with a feverish shiver, and for a second, the heart stopped dead.

It was the onset of fear.

During all the days and nights of sneaking and stealing past fields and villages, past abandoned hamlets and barely discernible footprints on side paths, the handful of Jews who now rambled through the woods in the gloomy autumn night had known no fear. It was haste in "bolting" from an apparent danger; it was tired despair, when with the little dose of poison in one's hand it seemed that any minute now it would all be over, the end—the enemy is near you and will soon grab you by the throat. But there was no fear.

The fear came here, in the thick forest, from the mere thought that there was nowhere left to go. It came here, when from between the mass of alder trees there came a flash of whiteness from a birch, when from somewhere fluttered the wings of a raven that while dozing had sensed the nearness of men. And the deeper they went into the darkness of the forest, the more often they would come to a halt as if by command, straining their ears to make sure they heard nothing, and then keep moving.

All at once they dropped to the ground and flattened out, again as if by command. Everyone's heart stopped beating. They buried their glowing breath in the damp moss, which responded with tepid warmth. And thus they remained until the reverberations of heavy steps, somewhere close by, had completely passed. They remained lying there in the same spot. They edged closer to each other—someone covered another's shoulder, and someone else's tired, heavy head fell near his neighbor's feet.

Only then, little by little, did regret begin to pierce them, for having lost the opportunity they had in fact been seeking for entire days and nights. For who could step so solidly in the depths of the forest at night, if not their own people, the sought-after and longed-for? Wasn't this the only wisecrack that people in the ghetto would repeat a dozen times, and always with pleasure: "Between the Germans and the forest-folk there is a pact—the day belongs to the Germans, the night to the partisans." Whenever the Germans would set out at night to reconnoiter, everyone knew that in order to tamp down their own fear they would raise such a racket that people kilometers away were warned.

Nevertheless, the slight tremor never left anyone's body for a moment. It was the fear of that which was one meter away from the group of Jews; of the foreignness of all these large and small trees surrounding them; of the shuddering loneliness of being no longer accompanied by anything, not even mortal danger. . . .

That same fear raised the handful of Jews again from their spot and commanded them to keep going, to trudge through the dreadful pathless forest, not knowing where it might lead them.

In stuttering blasts, like a face-to-face exchange of automatic weapon fire, came the shouting questions and answers when they suddenly bumped into a patrol.

"Stop! Who goes there? . . . Password!"

"We . . . We are Jews . . . ."

"Stretch out on the ground. . . . still as a corpse. . . When the chief comes, we'll sort it out."

So the men lay again on the ground, again buried their glowing breath in the damp, muddy grass. And they would not even lift their heads when they sensed hovering over them the patrol, who in a warm, humane tone requested:

"Check your pocket, dear brother; maybe a wad of tobacco will shake out . . . ."

A dead weariness spilled over their limbs. Soon they fell into a stupor that liberated everyone of everything; the fear evaporated. There remained the patrol, who listened to the deadened surroundings and to the carefree snoring of a handful of Jews who, after wandering and searching, had found true rest.

Historical Notes: *Smolar himself spent 17 days wandering in the forest after fleeing the ghetto: "We wandered for seventeen days and nights, got lost, but never gave up the search. On several occasions, we stumbled on Nazi search parties and drew our weapons to give battle. Finally we came upon some small partisan bands returning from diversionary missions" (RM 1966, 65). He wryly notes, "Thus it came about that after having provided thousands of Jews with guides or with detailed maps into the forests, we five set out 'to look for the wind in the field,' as the Russian saying goes" (TMG 1989, 112).*

Right Inside the Ghetto

The first to be taken out of the battle line was Leybl Tsukerman. The enemy's dumdum bullet hit him in his right hand. After him, Yitskhok Botvinik was killed. He was accompanying a newly-arrived group of partisans from the ghetto. They were intended to be formed into a new partisan company named after Kaganovitsh. When the enemy attacked the group, Yitskhok Botvinik defended them, giving them an opportunity to retreat. From his automatic weapon (which he had put together himself from bits and pieces assembled over a period of months), he let loose one blast of bullets after another. He shot without stopping, even when he was lying wounded on the ground. The last bullet he had reserved for himself, as was the habit of partisans.

Nokhem Goldzak was left alone with his plan, which was that together they should go to the ghetto and there, right there, carry out the diversionary work. This was no mere caprice—it was a personal desire to hurt the Hitler-enemy, in the very place where he wanted to exterminate all the Jews. And one more thing: Let the noise of the explosions lift the spirits of those who remained in the ghetto, and be a signal to them that they should escape the restraints and fulfill the great act of justice—vengeance!

When the commander of the partisan company appointed Nokhem as the senior leader of a demolition group, Nokhem decided: Now was the best time to realize Yitskhok Botvinik's, Leybl Tsukerman's and his, Nokhem's, dream.

Into his diversionary group he brought Tsilye, who had successfully made six trips on foot from the forest to the ghetto and back again with important Division communiques. He also took the young White Russian Vitke Rudovitsh into the group. Vitke's parents neighbored the ghetto. Joining the group as well was the company's singer,

Nokhem Elye. (In the forest there was hunger, it was cold, the enemy lurked on all sides—and whenever they had a minute of rest, the fighters would gather together in a dirt cave and Nokhem Elye would "read" Sholem Aleichem and Peretz. He had an ironclad memory, this former Mir yeshiva boy and later revolutionary. Whenever Nokhem Elye showed up at a peasant hut, the entire village would flock there. Everyone already knew: now there'd be a real show.) The partisans set off together, as had been agreed. At the Tatar cemetery, not far from the ghetto, the group halted; Tsilye left to reconnoiter, and all that was left to do was to "give a little push" in the most sensitive spot—by the railway semaphore.

That night, when Nokhem's mine took down from the railroad tracks forty cars loaded with the enemy's tanks, no one in the ghetto could sleep any longer. People who came to the woods later recounted: This was one of the rare happy nights for the prisoners of the ghetto.

Having rested up a bit, Nokhem's demolition group went on in the same direction, and again, a kilometer outside the ghetto, destroyed ten railroad cars. The scout reported the results precisely: fifty-four dead and forty severely wounded Hitlerists. In addition, on the railroad tracks there was left a large heap of broken anti-aircraft artillery and sappers' tools.

For a third time, the group set off on a perilous venture (for partisan explosives teams, it was second nature to take risks): They took a wagon into the city in broad daylight. They had loaded the wagon with hay, potatoes, some poultry, and eggs. They had hidden the explosives in the potatoes. Just then bad luck befell them—in the middle of the road the horse became unhitched. Hitlerists passing by shouted at them not to block the way. Everything hung by a thread. But as it was said, those who lay mines love to play with the devil himself, and right there in his very own hidey-hole. They pulled up close to the Jewish cemetery. They took a short rest with some acquaintances of Vitke Rudovitsh, and, reinvigorated, set off to do their work.

The crash of the train exploding that night drove the Hitlerists to a particular fury. At the same time, other vengeance-seekers did away with the Nazi chief executioner of the area. Nokhem, however, knew nothing of all this. Having taken the risk—"Let's go all the way": Right after the explosion he sent Tsilye and Vitke off to the ghetto to fetch everything that was needed for the division, and to bring new people back with them to the forest. Early the next morning, the ghetto was surrounded on all sides by police and gendarmes. But the partisans had successfully finished their work, and returned to the woods.

Historical Notes: *Strauss-Marko describes Smolar setting off on a mission with a group of four partisans, one of them being Nokhem Goldzak (Strauss-Marko 1983, 96-97).*

Nokhem Goldzak survived the war, went to Israel to fight in its War of Independence, and finally moved to Colombia, dying there in 1955 (Heller 1968, 596). In an article written by Goldzak before his death, "Lukover partisaner in di vaysrusishe velder" (492-494), Goldzak describes how, after fleeing Nazi-occupied Łuków to Minsk and subsequently being in the ghetto, he, Smolar and several others worked to create a new partisan unit and take Jews out of the ghetto and into the woods.

The Red-headed Miller

In the ghetto, among ourselves, we used to call him "the Red-headed Miller." We knew that this was a man from a small town somewhere, who had literally fled from the grave and come to us with just the shirt on his back. We could tell that he'd been a redhead from the few strands of red hair that were shot through his ash-gray beard. As to his having been a miller, this nobody knew. His thick brows, eclipsing his greenish eyes, looked as if they were always sprinkled with rye flour. How he had found out about us members of the underground, no one knew. He would shadow our footsteps, get to the gathering places of those who wanted to go off to the partisans, park himself in a corner, and be silent. With this stubborn silence, he got his way. We sent him off in in one of the first groups to a partisan division.

We'd forgotten all about the "Red-headed Miller." Then, in one of the brief letters we received from the forest, they wrote to us:

"The 'Red-headed Miller' (it seems that the partisans called him that too) sends his regards. He's become quite talkative. Send us more guys like him."

"An excellent fellow," we thought to ourselves as we read. "The man must certainly have left behind grandchildren in the pit in his hometown...."

The partisan company to which the "Red-headed Miller" belonged had been attacked at Rudinsk, by a Hitlerist penal division—some seven hundred handpicked criminals. The partisan company took up a defensive line. The "Red-headed Miller" stretched out near a pine tree, laid out his bullets, loaded his rifle, and started counting:

"This one is yours, murderer, for my devoted wife Sore, may she rest in peace"—and a Hitler youth is left lying to the right of the miller's pine tree.

"And this one is for you, my eldest daughter, Khane"—and again a killer is cut down.

"For my son, for Nosn, woe is me . . . ."

"For Leah . . . for Etl . . . for Beyltshe . . . ."

* *
*

Three times the "Red-headed Miller" reloaded his rifle. (These small-town Jews, as everyone knew, had big families.) He sees nothing of what is happening around him; each time he simply seeks a new target, and he shoots and scores a hit.

The "Red-headed Miller" feels someone tugging on his foot.

"Redhead!" Shouting at him, face already turning red, is his company commander. "Crawl back on all fours, so you're not stuck here. An order was given—pull back!"

"Wait a minute!" And the redhead busies himself once again with his rifle, manages to get it loaded a fourth time, and whispers, sending his bullet into a sixteenth fascist:

"This is in honor of you, may you live many long years, commander over all commanders, Comrade Stalin . . . ."

"From then on," says the letter from the forest, "the 'Red-headed Miller' became quite talkative."

Historical Notes: *It is only in this story and in "Partisan Bookkeeping"—both stories from the later, 1952 edition—that Stalin's name is mentioned at all, let alone in praise. There is no mention of Stalin in the 1948 Łódź edition. Both of these stories originally appeared in Smolar's* Fun Minsker geto, *published by the Soviet organ* Der Emes *in Moscow in 1946.*

The Debt Made Good

Yisroel Pogorelits cautiously grasped his commander Dakhno by the sleeve and softly but firmly whispered, so the others wouldn't notice:

"Enough, Commander. We don't know these people. After all, there are enemies about...."

Dakhno did not even glance in Yisroel's direction. With spiteful disdain he turned his back on him, lifted his head with the large white fur hat towards the ceiling, and sat there for a moment. Then he clasped his glass of vodka in both hands and, without taking a breath, tossed it down his throat. Having chased it with a bit of onion, he once more raised his head and remained sitting in that position until his eyelids began to droop. Suddenly, as if recalling some great necessity, he turned to Yisroel, fixed his greenish eyes on him and, drained as he was from great exertion, began to giggle hoarsely:

"You threaten little children ... enemies about ...."

Enraged, he leapt up, and shoving his hand against Yisroel's chest shouted out with rage:

"Here is the enemy—you! You!...."

Yisroel reached for his pistol, but quickly refastened his holster and slowly pushed Dakhno away, who made no effort to stop him.

The householders of the little hut clustered fearfully around the large oven, expecting a shootout to begin at any minute. Yisroel told them to get back to work, explaining: "Look—we'll just rest a bit here, and then be on our way."

Spent, Dakhno fixed his glazed eyes on Yisroel and good-naturedly appealed to him:

"Enough, my Pogorelitshik, enough. Better, let's have a drink together to brotherhood. Tomorrow may never come...."

Yisroel poured out two shots, and without a word brought his to his lips.

"Hold on a second," Dakhno stopped him: "You don't really mean this seriously...."

"Why, Commander?"

Dakhno set his glass back down:

"You're sly ones, you Jews. But you won't put one over on me. If we are brothers, then tell me: Why didn't Leybshteyn want to go with me? Eh? Why did Shafran spend so much time pleading his case before the commissar, and finally go off with Petshore's group, eh? And you, why have you come to me, of all people?"

Yisroel knit his brow. The Jewish partisans did indeed avoid Dakhno. They had no love for him. And he himself, Pogorelits, had come to Dakhno in order to show the group that they were wrong, that one would fare no worse with Dakhno than with any other commander. But what did this have to do with Dakhno's suspicion that he was the enemy?

"Don't play the fool. Perhaps you're going to say you don't even know who I am?"

"What do you mean?" Yisroel asked in surprise. "Of course I know. You're the commander of the Fourth Diversionary Detachment, which has already destroyed six German trains and is now going for the seventh...."

"Oh, cut it out," Dakhno interrupted his speech in a rage. "Don't give me that. You know very well the story about the fake letter 'D' that made me, the flesh and blood grandson of Batko—'Father'—Makhno, into the anonymous Dakhno. You hate me for my grandfather's sins, and your people have sent you to destroy me...."

Yisroel was not even aware of stepping away from Dakhno. Eyes opened wide, he stared at his commander as if he were seeing him for the first time. And he saw a face which was as much filled with pain as with vexation. Dakhno pushed away the shot glass, which wobbled on the table from the trembling of his nervous hands. No longer to Yisroel but to himself, he proclaimed:

"All my life I've been running from the memory of my grandfather.

The village that was my home, which as a child I left together with my parents, I haven't seen to this day, and here, precisely here, where our lives hold the same worth, you persecute me . . . no, I won't pay for Batko's crimes—do you hear me, Jew?"

"You will pay, you will pay, Commander," Yisroel murmured heatedly right into Dakhno's ear: "You will pay, not with seven, but with seven times seven trains of our common enemy. And I, the Jew Yisroel Pogorelits, will help you with that, and then we'll be even . . . ."

Without saying a word, both of them drained their glasses and began waking the rest of the group of partisans, to prepare to get underway.

* * *

Early mornings, when the full detachment was being assembled for daily formation, many of the partisans would typically have to be dragged out by the feet from their warm cots. This time, however, no one remained in the dirt cave. The word had arrived during the night, and no one had had any rest.

Standing before the detachment commander, before all the partisans lined up in rows, Yisroel reported:

"The diversionary detachment under the leadership of Commander Aleksander Dakhno destroyed one of the enemy's trains, consisting of twenty-four railroad cars filled with armament. In the course of defending his unit and ensuring a secure retreat, and above all, liberating the partisan Yisroel Pogorelits, who was surrounded by the enemy, perished heroically Commander Aleksander Dakhno, whose true family name was Makhno."

Afterwards came a warm word from the commissar, and finally the order that the partisan Yisroel Pogorelits be appointed the commander of the Fourth Diversionary, named after the heroic commander Aleksander Makhno.

Historical Notes: *The grandfather mentioned in the story is Nestor Ivanovych Makhno (1888–1934), known as Batko Makhno (from*

Ukrainian "Father Makhno"). Makhno was a Ukrainian anarchist revolutionary and the commander of the Revolutionary Insurrectionary Army of Ukraine from 1917–21, commonly known as the Makhnovshchina ("Makhno movement"). The Makhnovshchina, primarily composed of peasants, was widely rumored to have conducted pogroms, although the claims remain undocumented.

According to Skirda, Nestor Makhno had a daughter, Elena Nestorovna Mikhnenko. Both she and her mother, Halyna Kuzmenko, were persecuted by the Soviet government after WWII. She died unmarried in exile in Kazakhstan in 1993. Childless, she is quoted as saying, "I never wanted children. Bring more wretches into this world?" (Skirda 2004, 409)

The Concert

To the memory of Nokhem Elye Kagan

Thirty years Khil Arnshtam had spent in this world, traveled the length and breadth of it, and in all that time had never noticed one small detail: in order to place a horse collar on an equine throat, one must first turn it—the collar—face down, and only then tighten it into place.

Khil stood and pulled the collar forcibly, insistently, as a crowd of partisans around him shouted with ever-louder mocking laughter. It was no longer just cutting remarks; pieces of frozen snow began to fly at him. This further agitated the horse, which began to kick and rear his head so that Khil's hands could no longer reach it. Khil prepared to release his pent-up fury on the first person that came near him.

That person happened to be the good-natured Yanuk, second machine gunner in his detachment. Khil's rage began to ebb away, leaving him with a sense of utter impotence.

Then did Yanuk, unnoticed, using one hand only, turn over the collar and skillfully place it on the horse's neck. Then, just as unnoticed, did he blend back into the crowd that would have stood there for hours relishing Khil's despair.

When Khil came into the general staff's cave to report that the sled was ready for the journey, he encountered all the detachment commanders there. Before the chief of staff could order him to clear out, a few of the commissar's words reached him, unsettling him completely:

"The main thing is harmony—a true concert! One begins, the rest of them support...."

Khil could not restrain himself, and against all rules of partisan discipline cried out:

"Comrade Commissar, I am a musician by trade, ask me!"

With a burst of laughter, muffled by the deaf dirt walls of the cave, all faces turned in Khil's direction. Someone tossed off the remark, "Probably plays as well as he drives," and Khil quickly left the staff cave.

Ever since joining the partisan detachment, Khil had been dogged by one failure after another. Each of his ghetto comrades had settled in there, found his place. Only he, no matter what he undertook, could never pull it off. Already the partisans whose cave he shared avoided him, thought him a good-for-nothing and a braggart. Only one person, Yanuk, showed him a bit of compassion, and even that was probably out of pity.

Then one time his detachment surrounded a village where a police post had made its nest. Arriving in the village, they unleashed their fury on the police building, dispatched the few Ukrainian soldiers who had not yet managed to abscond, and then spread out among the huts to search for those in hiding. Khil entered a house that seemed a palace compared to the village huts. For a moment he stood dumbfounded, not even noticing the old noblewoman who in desperate fear murmured a prayer with trembling lips. Nor did he notice the young girl who clung to the old woman with all her might, in terror of being torn away. In a corner, Khil caught sight of a piano. With outstretched pistol in hand, he rushed towards it. Only then did he turn his head. Seeing the young girl, he quietly asked her:

"You will permit me?"

Stunned, she could not utter a word. Khil carefully raised the lid and passed his hands over the keys. The room soon filled with sounds, out of which a song began to grow, here carrying a turbulent anger, there becoming gentle, caressing—in order to shift quickly into a shrieking wail, a menacing exhortation.

Khil felt someone dragging him by his rifle. Looking around in confusion, he grabbed the bolt, ready to start firing rounds. He recognized Yanuk, and slowly Yanuk's soft reproach began to sink in:

that *Now is not the time,* that *police are hiding here,* that he will one day again *give concerts.*

Khil's feet seemed made of lead. His whole body was in turmoil. For a long time on the way back he spoke not a word. When he had fallen far behind his group, Yanuk waited for him, and only then did Khil let loose his tongue and speak of all the silent years in the ghetto and the forest. And Yanuk listened, only warning from time to time, "Look out, a hole."

"And this is how it is, even now. In everything around us, there is music, there is sound; it radiates truth as well as deception. You remember how they took me for a madman that night we heard over the camp the distant hum of an airplane motor, and I shouted for them to send up a flare. It was one of ours, I tell you a thousand times, ours! Such sounds can only be emitted by an instrument when operated by refined hands and an honest heart. Do we not recognize in the enemy's machine gun fire the cackling of a jackal, and in each of our shots the harmonious striking of a piano key? Oh, one must have an ear to perceive the truth in sound! Isn't the purpose even of today's 'operation' the striving for harmony, so that no alien sound should invade our lives?

"They led Jews of our town to the train—to the 'resettlement,' they called it. We musicians were placed up in front and ordered to play. We had to play a merry tune. And we played . . . and many felt it . . . and how they felt it! You see for yourself—we even found the way here . . .

"It is the power of sound, of true, authentic sound . . ." and all the firmer became Khil's and Yanuk's steps.

*   *
*

Divided into three groups, the partisans set off on different paths. They knew they were to meet at one spot, and then the "concert" would begin.

"May it go well!" the commander said to each and every one.

Not far from the railroad embankment they lay, and all around was quiet, just as if there were not hundreds of battle-ready and life-eager men, but only scattered rows of frozen stiff corpses.

Khil proved entirely incapable of containing his growing impatience. He cautiously turned on his side and bent over to Yanuk's ear.

"Do you hear it?"

Yanuk's frost-rimed brows lifted in an astonished questioning.

"It's already begun . . . in our hearts . . . the overture, I mean."

A bright rocket sliced through the sky, and after it—coming from several directions and aiming at one point—short blasts of machine gun fire rapped out in rhythm. Soon these were interrupted by long series of whistling bullets.

"Like dogs—do you hear a howling?"

Everyone rushed, half crawling, to the railroad tracks. Quickly they came up on the embankment, and the concert began.

To the accompaniment of gunpowder explosions, the rails—first one by one, then many—went flying into the air. As each rail exploded upward, the silhouette of the railroad tracks could be clearly seen, lit by a flash that illumined the entire stretch of sky. Falling back down, some of the rails gave a thin, rallying sound, lifting the partisans' spirits even more.

Khil's exploded rail lay somewhere below. Buried deep in snow, he burst forth in a rush of exuberance to find somewhere a "free" rail and try once again to hear the music of holy destruction. Then someone grabbed him by his fur coat.

"We must stay still! Watch the conductor. You're a musician, right?"

In the bright reflection of a flying rail, Khil recognized the commissar. He tried to pull back, but he could not. All the mightier became the symphony of light and sound. Noticing a group of fighters that, like him, was "out of work," he suddenly began conducting with his hands. A chant—at first scarcely audible, then more and more vigorous—began to clearly resound along the full length of the demolished railroad line.

Historical Notes: *Smolar dedicates this story to his comrade, writing "The death of our good friend Nochem Elya Kagan was a terrible blow to all Jewish partisans in the Frunze brigade." Tall, blonde, with an Aryan appearance, "Nochem Elya the Bundist, from the shtetl of Mir, knew entire stories of Peretz from memory." Kagan often cheered up his unit with Yiddish songs, poems and stories. The "kind, good-natured always helpful Nochem Elya was shot in the forest by a rabid anti-Semite named Baranowski, who turned out, upon investigation, to be an agent the SS had sent in to spy on the partisans. The death sentence we carried out on this murderous traitor did nothing to ease our pain" (TMG 1989, 126-127).*

A brief mention of "Nokhem Elye Kagan, the Bundist orator," is also found in Goldkorn (Goldkorn 1973, 200).

Partisan Bookkeeping

Generally, one shot from a rifle could be happenstance. A second—you're compelled to prick up your ears, strain your eyes, and at the same time make sure that your rifle is in your hands. A third—oh, a third shot has made matters clear, it means:

"Alert! Prepare to fight!"

The command duty officer that day, in the partisan camp of the 208th Detachment in Stalin's name, was the commander of the machine gun company Boris Khaymovitsh. Even before the messenger from "Secret" had come running up to report to Boris that the enemy was near, that he was approaching the camp, Boris had already succeeded in getting everyone on their feet, and he, along with his company, had left in the direction of the nearby village from which the enemy had attacked. A hail of bullets rained down on the partisan company. Boris gives the order: "Attack!" A bitter life-or-death battle ensues. The unit's political commissar is cut down. Near Boris, the partisan with the heavy machine gun falls down dead. Boris orders: "Forward! Smash these sons of bitches!" He himself lies wounded; he can't move. The commander of the Fourth Division, Shukalkin, made his way to him, so he could drag him out of the fire. But Boris keeps on shouting: "Advance! Slaughter the murderers!"

The Hitlerists were smashed in battle. They retreated in panic. Boris was brought to camp unconscious. When Grishka Gordon stepped up to his first surgical operation (Grishka became a "doctor" while still in the ghetto, although he had only managed to finish three courses at the medical institute), Boris looks at him with a pair of melancholy-smiling eyes (although his teeth are clenched together from pain) and boosts his courage:

"Be bold, dear brother; this isn't the way they cut us before...."

"When?"

"You've forgotten already? Right then, in the ghetto when the yellow star was sewn onto our clothing, then it cut ... it cut right into our hearts. I'll certainly feel no greater pain than that ... Now *they* will be feeling it ...."

The sedate, always deliberate Boris would lose all of his commander's composure when from somewhere nearby he detected a too-long blast of machine gun fire. Then he would switch over into battle mode! And it would always go this way: Boris and his unit always in the lead, always in the most perilous place on the front line.

It was about two weeks after leaving the ghetto. The enemy had ferreted out the location of the partisan camp. They suddenly attacked the partisan posts, pelting them with grenades from many directions. The partisans set off to creep up on the assaulting enemy. Boris and his company headed out to about three kilometers from the camp.

One and a half kilometers from camp a second group of partisans sits hidden. The enemy attacks. Two hundred Hitlerists advance, armed with automatic weapons and grenades. Boris lets them come closer, extremely close—already now they're about seventy meters from the partisans crouched down in waiting. And here comes the urgent command: "Fire!" With the first volley, the enemy loses thirty wounded and killed. The enemy's lines falter. But then he recovers. Boris suddenly heads his company over to the group sitting closer to the camp. Once again, they let the enemy move closer, and again: "Fire!"

Boris memorized well the first numbers (he later lost count of the reckoning): seventy marauders done away with.

The partisan movement received an order from headquarters: Wipe out the Hitlerist garrison, which had entrenched itself in the village of S.

The enemy had reinforced his base with long-range firing positions, with four rows of barbed wire, with anti-tank trenches.

The company prepared themselves well to carry out the command from partisan headquarters. In the woods, they built a mock-up of the enemy's positions, and each team went over the exact parameters of their task. The company that Boris must take into battle was given the assignment: Deliver the main strike.

First to open fire was the partisan artillery (the division possessed six 45-millimeter artillery pieces and one 122-millimeter cannon). Boris and his company come closer, a hundred meters out from the enemy's position, and—"Charge!" Now the enemy's barracks are burning. Shie Shnitman has run ahead to some thirty meters from the enemy, and opens fire on the embrasure. Frankel silenced the Hitlerists' long-range firing position. Now partisans are in the garrison, clearing out what's left of the enemy. Later the Hitlerist air force came swooping in, but they only came upon a graveyard, not a garrison. The mission had been fulfilled. No more Hitlerist garrisons were ever set up in the village of S.

The enemy garrison in B. seriously impeded the partisans. Because of this garrison, it was very difficult for them to get to the railway line. The garrison had to be razed.

Three partisan companies set off to fight. Boris leads the first company. He goes directly to the bandits' nest; the remaining two companies move in from the sides. A hundred of the murderers are done away with. Two bandits are holed up in an attic; one of them is the fascist mayor. "Doctor" Gordon gets in close to them and tells them "amicably" to crawl on down. A second partisan moves towards them—the mayor shoots him. The phlegmatic Gordon, who just a minute before had picked up a grenade that the mayor had thrown and tossed it back to him, flies into a fury, sends an incendiary round into the attic, and roasts the fascist alive.

* * *

When Boris is swept up in the excitement, he often forgets to look around him and see whether the partisans from his company have managed to follow him.

The rendezvous with an SS company at the village of H. concluded with the gang of criminals being forced to retreat. Boris hunts them down. He fills the backs of four Hitlerists with bullets. Boris doesn't notice that only he remains: an order has been given to retreat. A Hitlerist has taken a position on the ground and aims his weapon at Boris. Boris drops to the ground, and a duel begins. Some ten minutes pass as they lie there, one against the other, seeking that instant when a well-placed bullet will put an end to the duel. Boris shouts (half in Yiddish, half in German): "Give yourself up, or I'll wipe you out on the spot." But the other stays hidden, waits until Boris runs out of bullets, and then begins edging closer to him. Who knows how the battle would have ended, had there not come clambering over to Boris the fourteen-year-old Mishke Bonitski. Together they did away with the fascist.

In battle it often happens this way: you want to meet face to face with the enemy (after the ghetto, this desire became second nature to the Jewish populace), and here you've been assigned instead to a supporting position.

The great battle of the rails began. Partisans were out on all the railway tracks in the country, to strike a single concentrated blow and destroy the enemy's communications. This was in preparation for the general assault by the Soviet army.

The partisans of the division to which Boris Khaymovitsh belonged are given an assignment: in one night's time, destroy two thousand rails. Boris and his group are ordered to protect the division from any unexpected attacks by the enemy. Nothing to be done about it, an order is an order!

The division does its job. Everyone is elated with their success. Boris goes about the camp upset; he can't seem to settle down. He speaks, makes his arguments to the headquarters team, and the next morning he and his company go off. To the general total of shattered rails, they brought their own contribution—five hundred and eighteen more pieces.

Two partisan divisions, among them Boris and his battle-comrades, receive a mission from headquarters: destroy the enemy's five trains. They head off to the area of the station. To make any movement along this railroad sector is tremendously difficult. The Hitlerists protect this line as if it were the apple of their eye. Nevertheless, the diversionary team succeeds in laying the detonation material. One train goes by—no explosion. New explosive material is placed. A second train goes by—nothing. A third, a fourth—just as if no mines had been laid. The day is dawning. They need to pull back immediately from the railroad lines. But another train comes flying by—quite an aristocratic one—and the entire area is deafened by a horrific explosion ("Surely this was heard in the ghetto," Boris thinks to himself). The enemy's air ambulances spent an entire day flying in and out, transporting the wounded and dead. They were, it seems, very "high ranking personages" (otherwise they would have been buried on the spot and not taken back by airplane). After this extremely successful operation, the two partisan groups knock down four more transports from the rails. Some sixty railroad cars with "live merchandise" and the enemy's war technology were completely obliterated.

Boris Khaymovitsh had long ceased to carry on his bookkeeping of acts of vengeance against the fascist beasts. With each new operation, he always felt as if he were starting right from the beginning.

Historical Notes: *Smolar was previously acquainted with Khaymovitsh and Shnitman before meeting them in the Minsk ghetto: "We ran into Boris Khaymovitsh often in the ghetto, and we knew—his mind was totally made up; he was ready to get right to work. With Shie Shnitman—the same" (FMG 1946, 21). He later mentions Boris Khaymovitsh, Shie (Isaiah) Shnitman, and Grishka Gordon multiple times, telling how in August 1941 he met "with two natives of Minsk—Boris Haimovich [sic], who was a former director of a large textile factory and a reserve officer in the Red Army, and Isaiah Shnitman, a textile worker" (TMG 1989, 29). Grishka Gordon is also found in the text, described as "a medical student, who became a highly capable partisan" (TMG, 64).*

Khaymovitsh was the commander of a machine-gun detachment in the 208th Brigade. Smolar's accounts of Khaymovitsh also appear in Moshe Kaganovitsh's Di milkhome fun di yidishe partizaner, *v. 2. Kaganovitsh first cites a description of Khaymovitsh as a fighter (TMG 1989, 81) put out by this same brigade, the "208th in the name of Stalin," that states: "Boris Feyvelevitsh (son of Feyvel) Khaymovitsh, born 1910, party comrade, was a model of heroism and daring during the years of fighting. He actively took part in forty partisan battles." Kaganovitsh later (TMG, 116) gives the names of the three villages in the story: Susha, Hatitsh, and Bahoshevitsh.*

Khaymovitsh survived the war: In the same book (TMG 1989, 153), Smolar writes of spotting him in Moscow on 16 July 1944, at the great parade of 30,000 partisans. Meeting at a "partisan village" after the parade, they had a chance to catch up. Smolar reflects: "I could not take my eyes off the sun-bronzed young face of Boris Haimovitsh [sic]. He was the only one left of the four friends with whom—on that Sunday in August 1941—I had begun the chapter of the resistance organization in the Minsk ghetto. And he was the first one to go out into the forest."

As a partisan with First Company, the Nineteenth Brigade (presumably a Soviet unit), Cholawski also tells of the "The Battle for the Railway Lines," an assault which ordered "every partisan brigade in the area to camp beside a different section of track and to plant mines." During his squad's mission the Germans detected their presence and opened fire, but they were able to return to safety. "As we retreated some hundred meters from the tracks, a long chain of explosions flashed behind us—mission accomplished" (Cholawski 1980, 175).

The first partisans from the Minsk ghetto, from right to left (first row): A. Relkin, F. Shedletski. Second row: G. Gordon, B. Khaymovitsh (Photographs from Smolar's Fun Minsker Geto*)*

פארטיזאנער פון מינסקער געטא

פון רעכטס אף לינקס (ערשטע ריי): ה. סמאליאר – קאמיסאר פון פאר־
טיזאנער־אטריאד "סערגיי לאזא", ש. זארין – קאמאנדיר פון אטריאד
נום. 106. ב. כאימאוויטש – קאמיסאר פון 1־טן אטריאד פון דער
208־טער בריגאדע. צווייטע ריי: נ. פעלדמאן – קאמיסאר פון פארטיזאנער־
אטריאד 25. יאר וסס"ר", וו. קראווטשינסקי – קאמאנדיר פון דער
דיווערסאנטנ־גרופע פונעם אטריאד אפן נאמען פונעם מארשאל בודיאני,
כ. פייגעלמאן – קאמיסאר פון אטריאד נום. 106.

Partisans from the Minsk ghetto

From right to left (front row) H. Smolar – commissar of Partisan Otriad "Sergey Lazo"; Sh. Zorin – commissar of the Otriad Num. 106; B. Khaymovitsh – commissar of the 1st Otriad of the 208th Brigade

Second row: N. Feldman – commissar of the Partisan Otriad "25 year VSSR"; V. Kravtshinski – commander of the Diversionary Group of the Otriad in the name of Marshal Budyonny; Kh. Feygelman – commissar of the Otriad Num. 106

The Family

No such command had been issued, and no one had ever considered who it was that had granted the family such unlimited rights. All the family moved freely throughout the villages and forests of the partisan zone, and it was enough that in response to the demanded password, the answer would come, "the Onion Folk." And with that they would be allowed to pass even into the sector headquarters.

No one ever called them by their real name. Not even the Jewish partisans, who knew that the old man was called Bere Leyb, that his wife's name was Sime, and that their son, aside from his nickname "a ruble and twenty" (he limped a bit on one foot), had such a fine-sounding name as Itshe Velvel. As to the little girl with the thin braids that were always tightly plaited across her small blond head, she was simply called "the youngest." Everyone, even the Jews, referred to them as nothing but "the Onion Folk."

As the old man Bere Leyb explained it one time over a drink, the nickname originated from his keeping kosher. As it happened, one could come to a friendly peasant in the village and be treated to "a glass of milk ... from a crazy cow" (moonshine, that is). To chase it down, the peasant would set out a few slices of dried sausage or some yellowed bacon. And Bere Leyb would turn his head away and entreat the master of the house: "A piece of onion will be plenty." Thus was acquired the nickname in which over time no hint remained of the original mockery: "the Onion Folk."

The dirt cave of Bere Leyb's family differed quite markedly from the usual partisan caves, which resembled barracks. The clay walls were covered with straw, from which a pleasant reflection would fall upon the surrounding darkness. In the kitchen, which had been hammered together from a tin gasoline barrel, hung a shelf of dishes that were always washed sparkling clean. The dirt floor was spread with pine branches that would fill the cave with the holiday scent of Sukes. No one had ever seen a weapon on the wall of Bere Leyb's cave or on a stand, as was typical among partisans. Yet they also knew that as soon as Bere Leyb happened to come across "a better piece," he would make an exchange and keep it himself. None of "the Onion Folk"—whether on the road or when arriving at a partisan base—could be observed with a weapon, although everyone was well aware, that each of them had hidden on them some sort of weaponry. "It's not fitting," Bere Leyb would say, who always, even in his dress, maintained the amicable appearance of a small-town Jew.

But anyone who saw "the Onion Folk" during a raid, when entire regiments of SS troops surrounded the forest and set about attacking the partisan brigades, would understand that *these* were the true "Onion Folk." Gone was the smile that always lay upon Bere Leyb's creased face. His small soft beard became tautly pointed, fusing itself completely to the grey mustache and eclipsing the tight seam of his lips. His cocked ears were the first to hear the command, and he was among the first to stretch out on the ground, his rifle aimed and ready. His wife Sime too, who was always falling behind on the road, unable to catch up to her "warriors," would suddenly lose her encompassing heavy roundness and nimbly manage to be by Bere Leyb's side. Of Itshe Velvel's lameness not a trace remained. With his automatic rifle across his chest, he did not even for an instant take his eye off "the youngest," who followed after him carrying a sack of loaded magazines for the rifle.

As soon as the raid was over, the family once again headed back to the old cave. If the cave was wrecked, like the majority of the partisan caves, the four of them would begin seeking out a new spot away from the nearby bases. There they would again dig out a cave that would possess the same feeling of home as so many others that had been destroyed, and once again take up the normal forest life of "the Onion Folk."

* *
*

A newly arrived Jewish partisan would be greatly irked by this. "How is it that they, the family, just go their own way? Why shouldn't they join a detachment like hundreds of others, and do what everyone else does?"

"They're the ones who give wicked tongues fodder for slander about us," such a one would say heatedly—until the time came when he would see for himself that in fact people everywhere held "the Onion Folk" in high esteem.

It had never happened that in the family's unattended cave, when Bere Leyb and his family were out on the road, anyone would allow himself, even in a drunken state, to enter and have the run of the place, or to take something from it.

It was to this place that they would come when they had a free minute and "the Onion Folk" were at home. They would bring along half a liter[1], a bit of cheese and butter, or something really good from a successful "bombing"[2] and present them as a gift to the lady of the house, or to "the youngest." They would come there to find out the latest news from Bere Leyb, who would cover a lot of ground, gather up the slightest rumor, and deliver it to the proper place. Then he would return, fill his lungs with the longed-for feeling of home, tear off a shirt already fallen to pieces, and receive a basin full of hot water from Sime, so that he might feel the pleasure of a clean-scrubbed body.

Yet the main reason people would come to the cave was with a hidden intention. The friendlier they became with the family, the more deeply they would be engraved in its memory, and with this they would gain the certainty that no matter what should happen, some recollection of them would remain—a trace of a life whose last moment had lain crouched and waiting at every step.

It had begun during the time when the forest did not yet have a

---

1. Refers to moonshine.
2. [Smolar's note] Requisition of property taken from hostile or wealthy elements.

master. Regular German military units still passed through the main road without fear.

On the side paths, small groups fleeing from captivity or from encirclement by the Germans would sneak out when the nights were pitch-black, to seek out a little food. People called them "partisans," but they were really people who, in desperation, sought a hiding place so as not to fall into the enemy's hands. One such group would avoid meeting another, suspecting every living person they met of bearing only death for them.

At that time, Bere Leyb had come to the woods neighboring his town, in order to find protection there for what remained of his family. Deadly peril lurked all around. One couldn't move about, and sitting in one spot was dangerous. Then the thought occurred to Bere Leyb that he could burrow underneath one of the hundreds of graves that had been hastily dug to cover the remains of fighters killed in battle. He would remain there during the daytime and then at night, either alone or with his youngest child, set out to the neighbors for a bit of food and water.

The grave proved to be a secure trench until the forest did acquire its master: true partisans, who showed up and mined all the roads, forcing the enemy to avoid the forest. Then Bere Leyb came out of his hiding place, and without asking anyone's leave and with the determination of one fulfilling a solemn vow, began together with his family to dig out the graves, transporting the remains of the battle-slain to a site deeper in the forest. Partisans would stop, look upon the work of the four "civilians" without asking any questions, and bid them farewell with a sympathetic word. Once a Jewish lad tried to toss off a mocking comment: "Apparently, Uncle, you were the president of the Burial Society." Bere Leyb answered him with his sad smile, which the young man understood to mean, "And who knows where your own bones will come to rest."

The general staff of the zone took an interest in the family. The partisans knew that "the Onion Folk" were providing weapons to the detachments. Rifles with rusted bolts and rotted wooden stocks, which since the beginning of the war had lain in the graves together with their onetime owners, began once again to serve skilled hands. The partisans even knew about an entire arsenal that someone had hidden in graves and disguised from above with crucifixes, and which the family had then uncovered.

Yet it was not of this that the partisan commander would whisper together with Bere Leyb for long hours. It was not even of the news that the family would bring with them from the wide world. It was instead a conversation on the age-old custom of not abandoning one's fallen brother to the enemy—a custom of which one was reminded day in, day out by the words of the battle command: "Eternal memory to the heroes who fell in battle for the just cause."

And when partisans would meet the family somewhere distant, close to the enemy's positions, they would know: these formidably peaceful people were heading for a difficult mission. And when they should return, they would bring with them all that was possible to bring of a fallen battle comrade. And above all they would bring peace to the spirits of the living, who—today, tomorrow, each and every day until victory was achieved—would be walking towards certain death.

The family strengthened the faith in the hearts of the living that they would never allow anyone to pass away in that traceless anonymity which is much more terrible than death.

Historical Notes: *Graves containing weapons buried along with their former owners were a grim resource for partisans desperate for weapons. Belarussian Jewish partisan Cholawski tells of local peasants reporting to his staff the discovery in the Kopyl region of a mass grave of Red Army soldiers, buried along with their weapons. "This was in accordance with the Germans' mocking custom of demonstrating their contempt for the Red Army by not deeming it worthwhile to gather up the spoils of war, but instead burying the soldiers with their guns." The work was psychologically taxing: he describes how he, as part of a large group of Jewish men, went up to the grave that night. They opened the grave and began pulling out "from in between the bodies, the long clumps covered with sticky soil. The terror of death and the guilt of sacrilege enveloped us" (Cholawski 1980, 94).*

The Night of the White Devils

That the brigade was planning to accomplish something extremely important, one could easily surmise. All the units and groups were energetically preparing themselves. They cleaned the weapons, dried off the bullets, oiled the bolts. Women prepared bandages, sewed camouflage garments, readied biscuits. Only the small fry wandered about underfoot awaiting an errand, watching for a rider to come flying up so they could grab his horse to unsaddle it and toss it a bit of hay or some chopped straw. The commander issued an order: several boys were to be added to every patrol. Although the frost was severe, the gang accepted the order with joy: as if it were a small thing, to receive a rifle in one's hand!

The detachment commander was already aware of the brigade commander's directive that on the appointed night when they must attack the enemy, no one able to fight should remain on base. Indeed, for that reason, the commander had decided to get the young ones accustomed to the fact that on that night they would guard the entire base by themselves. Gradually, without any sort of official order, a children's group came into being within the detachment. One of the perpetual jokesters had dubbed this group "The Snotnoses." The inspiration for this nickname was nine-year-old Mikhke, a robust boy who ate enough for three and whose strength was no less than that of an adult, but whose nose was always running.

The boy in charge of the group—although no one had designated him as such—had come to be Vitke, a short, thin lad who despite his fourteen years looked no older than Mikhke. Vitke could shoot an automatic rifle; he bragged that he could already be a number one gunner with the "Maxim" machine gun. And this was quite possible: he knew the parts of the Maxim by heart. He had another virtue: he could ride like the best cavalryman. With or without a saddle, Vitke would seem to be fused to the horse; it made no difference whether the horse was at a gallop or a fast trot.

As his "commissar," Vitke had chosen "Comrade Yako-Tako." It was with this name—*jako-tako* meaning "so-so" in Polish—that the gang had crowned twelve-year-old Arek, who if you asked him in the morning, "How did you sleep?" had only one answer: "Oh, yako-tako." If you asked him after lunch whether he was full, again he would answer, "Oh, yako-tako."

He became "commissar" because no one in the whole squad could match his expertise in telling stories. When the gang would sit down at the campfire or at the small stove burning in the earthen cave and Arek would begin telling one of his dozens of stories, the older partisans, as if for no particular reason and without facing Arek, would edge up closer and listen quietly until the end of the story.

To the gang's "staff" also belonged Yoshke "Potato." His job was to furnish all those going out on patrol with full pockets of potatoes, to fortify their souls through the long winter night. It was the kitchen detail that had given him that fine name.

All told, the group was comprised of seventeen youths. There were still other children in the detachment, almost all of them rescued from the ghetto. But they were either still very small or simply of no use to Vitke, and he ordered them to sit in the caves.

The evening before the squad was to march out, it became especially quiet on the base, although there were more people present than usual. Everyone who was still on the road for a military operation, an economic mission, or a lecture in the villages, had received an order to return quickly to base. People were doing everything more carefully, more calmly than normal, although inwardly each one was seething with excitement, awaiting the difficult and dangerous fight. It was as if in the stillness they wanted to conceal even more securely from the enemy's eye the secret of the coming battle.

In this same quiet manner, one unit after another left the base. It seemed that even the horses' hooves clopped more softly against the frozen ground. Without any screeching, the one and only artillery piece also departed. As had been decided, there remained on the base a duty officer in charge, the selected group of youths, and the women (except for the female medics) with the rest of the children.

When the detachment had vanished completely into the darkness of the early winter dusk, a dreadful emptiness descended on the camp. Vitke positioned the watch patrol at their posts. He gathered the remainder of the group together in one cave, and bade them lie down for a nap until their turn came to relieve the watch. But no one could shut their eyes. So one by one they dragged themselves down from their sleeping places, sat down next to the small glowing stove, and listened intently to the quiet of the night.

Vitke got up from the stove, pulled on his fur coat, and made for the exit.

"If you want, come with me," he called from the door to Yoshke. "I'm going to check in with the watch."

Everyone jumped up from their places, and began to put on their coats and leave the cave. Vitke, in the manner of a boss, gave them merely a stern glance but spoke not a word. He himself could not just sit in the cave—should he order them to do so?

A little way down the road Yako-Tako, the sergeant of the guard, met them with his loud, shrill cry: "Stop! Who goes there?"

"Seventeen," Vitke answered.

"Minus three," Arek responded sternly, according to the established password.

The gang piled into the dark, cold guard-cave, where a few coals barely smoldered. They huddled together closely and soon felt more encouraged and at ease. Whispering quietly, they slowly began to talk about where the detachment might be at that moment, approximately when the storm would begin, and whether they would hear it when the "Katyusha" (that was the sole artillery piece) began to roar. Although "Yako-Tako" was also there in their midst, today it did not occur to anyone to ask him to tell one of his stories. The conversation turned to news of the different detachments, of their accomplishments and clever stratagems. The boys also told of happenings in the surrounding area. From the overheard conversations of the grown-ups, the gang had precise knowledge of all the neighboring villages and cities, knew where our people were located and where someone else's, the good and the bad, where the German garrisons and the police garrisons were, how big they were, and what kind of weapons they had.

And when all the news had been exhausted, "Yako-Tako"—unusually, without being asked—began to tell a story. And the story was especially suited to everyone's mood, to everyone's restlessness which did not allow them to shut their eyes. It was the story of "the little red devils," the little brother and sister who set out to find their father, managed to get inside the enemy's camp, and caused great trouble for those relatives of the present-day Germans; they battered them left and right. And all this from just the two of them—two children.

Vitke got up from his place even before Arek had finished the story, ostensibly to check on the watch. When he came back to the cave, several voices were engaged in a quiet dispute: whether one could—without the commander's permission—set out, just like those "little red devils," to a garrison somewhere, do a bit of damage, and then disappear.

"Because what are we going to accomplish by sitting here, what?" concluded Shimke the shepherd (in the summer he was the chief overseer of the cows).

"Three men on the watch are enough. So why do the rest of us, every last one, need to sit here telling each other stories?"

From the half-secret whispering it became noisy in the cave. Everyone's voices blended into one argument: Something had to be done! In the commotion, Vitke managed to drag Arek outside unnoticed, and then Yoshke. They hid themselves under a spreading pine tree, and there in quiet secrecy they decided:

They would pick—in addition to themselves—five of the most agile boys, take along two guard-rifles plus sticks and knives for everyone, and without giving those remaining behind any sort of explanation, pretend they were returning to the base. As Vitke began laying out the order of the watch for the entire night—who was to relieve whom—Yoshke went quickly back to the base to gather up sheets, shirts, towels—everything that might be of use.

"If anything happens, let me know," Vitke instructed those remaining in the cave to finish out the night watch. Then he set out at once at the head of the group that, wrapped in white, cautiously slipped out toward the horizon.

* * *

The joy of the great victory over the enemy garrison in the town of M. evaporated as soon as the weary returning partisans learned that there was no trace of Vitke, Arek, Yoshke and the rest of the "Snotnoses." It was not just for the boys that the commander was concerned. Could the enemy, at the same time that they had defeated him at one point, have managed from a second position to get here, to their base, and seize the children? It didn't make sense, though—why hadn't he touched the guard patrol or the duty officer, why hadn't he carried off the women and children? As dead tired as they all were, several riders immediately volunteered to reconnoiter, in order to find the tracks of the boys.

Not an hour had passed when one of the scouts reported that at the second kilometer the snow was trampled by a large number of riders, as if a whole squadron had stood there.

The commander immediately ordered an alert. The partisans' hearts felt as if they had quickly filled with fresh blood, leaving them as refreshed as if they had not just spent an entire night conducting a perilous battle against the enemy. The units were deployed in different directions along the edge of the forest, in order to defend all fronts. In the middle of the base was placed the "Katyusha," which had scarcely two rounds remaining.

In tense expectation, those lying in wait along the northern border of the woods picked up the sound of horses heavily treading. They immediately sent word to the commander, and scouts on horseback were dispatched in that direction. But before any reports had been sent back, through the very depths of the mud—which often did not freeze all winter—there crawled out with great effort a filthy individual on a horse, and after him a second, a third. Tattered, muddied pieces of linen were tangled between their legs. The crowd of partisans began besieging them from all sides, realizing that "the treasure had been found."

"Tell us what happened!" the commander severely ordered the mud-covered boy, in whom it was barely possible to recognize the "commissar," "Yako-Tako."

Arek drew himself to attention in a soldierly fashion, boldly fixed his eyes on the commander, and with dignity replied:

"The operation was successful, Comrade Commander; all have returned to base intact. As to the rest, Vitke will give the report."

The commander's initial anxiety, which at the sight of the boys had passed into anger, began to get it off his chest with a good-natured mockery of "the heroes in the torn underpants." The camp became noisy again. People began dashing from one observation point to the next. A resounding hurrah greeted the arrival of a herd of cows and sheep, surrounded by riders seated on genuine cavalry saddles. In the lead rode Vitke in triumph, his rifle on his arm in the style of a real commander.

"Lay it all out, chief," the commander ordered good-humoredly.

Vitke drew himself up and began the report according to all the military standards customary among true partisan fighters:

"I understood myself that the lads were right. What would we accomplish sitting here at the base at a time when all of you were off fighting? The gang began to revolt. 'Yako-Tako' fanned the flames some more. He told a story that got everyone fired up. Might as well set right out into the world to fight the Germans. I know that one must not break any order from the commander . . . you entrusted the base to us . . . .

"Well, so we, eight of the nimblest boys, set off just exactly as you see us, in camouflage. We knew that in the village of Yavorshtshina the police had rounded up horses and cattle that they had plundered from the peasants. How many policemen were there, we didn't know, but we thought that if 'the little red devils' could set out against whole armies of Whites, we could certainly attempt it against a few Blacks. We also figured that when you began to attack in the town of M., and when our 'Katyusha' showed what she could do, Yavorshtshina would get raucous too, and then we would fall on the Black gang.

"And that was how it was. We walked one after the other, like geese. We avoided the hamlets, often crawling up to our necks in snow. No one made a sound. We took detours, covering extra ground. We got a little bit lost, and here you helped us. On one side of us, something started to burn; the sky turned red. So we realized in which direction we needed to go.

"When we got close to Yavorshtshina, I went ahead to scout around. I handed over the command to Arek. In case I got killed—let him lead. On all fours, I managed to reach the first huts—dead, silent. Everyone snoring. But where was the barn, the horses, the stables, the cattle? I sniffed it out. There, walking around, was a bundled-up man with a rifle. Near him shone a little kerosene lamp. This meant that the dogs were keeping watch.

"On the way back, I already had the plan ready. We all stretched out on the snow, a meter apart from each other, and lying there we waited for the 'Katyusha' to send us regards.

"We could see clearly how the policemen, in nothing but their underwear, started running back and forth as if they'd been poisoned. Then I ordered: let everybody in one row start rolling toward the base. It was a little tough to roll with the rifles. We shoved them down underneath the sheets. The nearer we got to the place, the more covered in snow we became; we turned into big balls of snow. When the police spotted the flying snowballs, they began to shout and scream as if they'd really gone crazy.

"As we'd agreed, four of us threw ourselves at their guard. Here, take a look at him, the fine gentleman. This is Yoshke's handiwork. He's the one who did such a nice job on him. The same four broke open the doors and began to drive out the horses and cattle. Meanwhile we set off after the policemen. They screamed; we made an even bigger racket. The 'Katyusha' helped us. All around, the sky was red. What we accomplished there, we don't know. Fishke's hand got covered with blood. He says he hit one of them in the snout with a knife, and one snagged a piece of his hand with his teeth. Arek also gave someone a caress. We didn't have much time. We merely made a quick search of the stable, where we picked out a few good saddles. We all mounted the horses and off we went—back home. Our plan was to come back before the whole squad returned. The blame, however, lies with the cows and the sheep. We had a nice bit of trouble herding them. And we didn't want to leave any tracks to our base. So we split up into three groups and decided to meet up at the second kilometer from the base. And that was what happened. Again, there was a problem. After all, we mustn't flatten out such a wide path straight over here. So we split up again, in order to come in from different directions, mainly through the mud...."

Vitke took a deep breath, quickly pulled himself to attention once again, and in an official tone concluded:

"I report to you, comrade commander, that last night the partisan unit under my command, numbering eight fighters, assailed the enemy's camp in the village of Yavorshtshina. As a result of a short battle, we forced the enemy to retreat. Among the enemy are dead and wounded; their number has not yet been ascertained. We seized four rifles and seven grenades. In addition to that, we took into custody one policeman. All of our fighters returned to base. We brought trophies: eight horses, five cavalry saddles, twelve cows, and several sheep. We lost some of the cattle along the way."

As Vitke finished his report, a heavy mist began issuing from the nostrils of many of the partisans, as if they had been holding their breath for a long time.

"Good," the commander answered quietly. "Now go, wash up, and lie down to rest. In the morning, get in formation with everyone else to listen to the daily orders. Oh, yes, and tell the kitchen supervisor to make a holiday lunch today. With a little bit extra. For the children, also a little...."

* *
*

The squad was lined up according to units. First in the row of the seventeen youths was Vitke, although according to his height he should have stood somewhere toward the back of the line.

The commander read out the daily orders. He detailed precisely the course of the combat operation against the enemy garrison in the town of M., the mistakes committed, the deficiencies noted. He listed the names of the heroic fighters, who were being thanked by the headquarters staff and designated to receive high combat distinctions.

In the second part of the daily orders were listed the accomplishments of the partisan group under the command of the leader Vitke (no one knew his family name, not even the commander). Precisely reported were the number of trophies and the manner in which the attack had been executed.

In the concluding section of the orders, it was announced:

"Taking into account the especial daring and heroism that the underage group of partisans demonstrated, and the significant results of their fight, it is decided to call upon the top command of the partisan movement to give high combat honors to all those who took part in the attack."

For a moment the commander lifted his eyes from the paper, glanced at the boys, and scanning every word, continued reading:

"Taking into account that the entire group left their posts on their own authority, thereby disobeying the commander's order to guard the base—all eight are punished with additional kitchen duty for two weeks."

From then on, all the boys of the squad were counted as full members in the ranks of the partisan fighting men.

Historical Notes: *The use of colors in "Red Devils" corresponds to the various warring sides during the Russian civil war (1918-1920): The Russian Red and White armies, and the Blacks, which refers to the Ukrainian anarchist forces. In this story, the mention of the Blacks is likely a reference to the WWII Nazis—with their black uniforms and swastikas—and their local allies.*

This story alludes to the book Red Devils, *written by Pavel Blyakhin in 1921 and made into a film in 1923, which features three youngsters who outwit the Ukrainian anarchist Nestor Makhno during the Russian Civil War.*

Shalom Cholawski, a Jewish partisan in the forests outside of Minsk, tells of a "number of unarmed Jewish youngsters" who were attached to an armed group of partisans making a raid on a collective farm. He tells how the "Jewish boys marched along under the cover of partisan guns; they had nothing to defend themselves with in the face of possible fire from the German watch. Nevertheless, that night, herds of cows and pigs were brought into the partisan camp" (Cholawski 1980, 92).

His Machine Gun

As the detachment went off to battle to crush the enemy's garrison in the town of Miadiel, Khayim Aleksandrovitsh was aware that there was one more objective in this fight—to liberate the Jews in the local ghetto. During this battle, Khayim manned the machine gun.

The enemy sensed the danger, and sent out an extra liaison officer to the neighboring garrison for help. With his machine gun, Khayim intercepted him mid-way.

The assault on the garrison began. Jews in the ghetto had been notified in advance that the hour of liberation approached. With taut nerves and pounding hearts they awaited the saviors, to unite with them in battle against the blood enemy. The battle lasted five hours. There were victims among the partisans. The detachment deputy commander had taken a bullet. Four partisans lay dead. The rage and determination grew stronger. Already the enemy's trenches were taken. Partisans had entered the town. They were still in the process of eradicating the last bandits of the Hitlerist garrison when Khayim and a group left for the ghetto with the joyous call of liberation, "Jews, come out of the ghetto!"

And out the Jews came. The young and battle-capable were immediately incorporated into the fighting ranks. The elderly, the women and children, were escorted into the forest to a family camp, from which they would later be sent off to the other side of the front lines.

Khayim shared in the great joy of their liberation, and at the same time was thinking about "his" ghetto: about his murdered wife, Mashe, about his little six-year-old daughter Noymele.

. . . And now it had to do with the number thirteen.

"It's my lucky number," Khayim had earlier responded to the wisecracking of his comrades over the "devil's dozen."

In camp, as usual, few people remained. Most left at night: some off on a combat operation, others on diversionary tactics, some off to reconnoiter, and others on a supply run, or to carry out propaganda work among the local populace. In Khayim's company, only five people were left, and suddenly—an alarm! The enemy is close by! Of the entire brigade, barely one hundred and twenty men remained. They called on the nearby detachment, and together mounted a defensive position. Khayim and his machine gun were on the right flank. Farther to his right were some thirty men from the neighboring unit. The left flank was working miracles, letting the enemy know who they were dealing with. The Hitlerists threw themselves to the right with heavy automatic weapon fire. Khayim readied himself to engage the enemy and just then, at the most critical moment—stop! The machine gun's magazine jammed. The Germans sensed the partisans' weak spot. They were now ten meters from Khayim. Cold-bloodedly (with that amazing cold-bloodedness that aside from Aleksandrovitsh, few others possessed), he took out the magazine, swiftly filled another with bullets, and literally at the very last second his machine gun started to chatter. Thirteen Hitlerists (the very thirteen that his friends had teased him about) lay dead from that first burst of bullets. The rest became disoriented. They rushed to one side, farther to the right, where the neighboring group lay. The group could not withstand the abrupt assault of the enemy. There was a danger that the Hitlerists would cut the partisans off from their return route.

Quietly, unnoticed, Khayim managed to approach them. Again his machine gun began rapidly to "stitch." The enemy retreated.

Historical Notes: *Kaganovitsh (Vol. 2 1956, 114-115) describes how Khayim Aleksandrovitsh, well-liked in his unit, quickly rose through the ranks of one of the most famous partisan brigades in Belarus (BSSR). He mentions that Aleksandrovitsh remarked to his comrades, after killing thirteen enemy in one fight, that the number thirteen had been lucky for him, thus earning the nickname "Khayim Draytsener" ("Khayim the Thirteener"). A version of this story also appears in the text.*

Kaganovitsh identifies the partisan base in the story as that of "Diadia

Vasia" ("Uncle Vasia"), and notes that Aleksandrovitsh and his machine gun, along with this brigade, later took part in the liberation of the Jews from the Miadiel ghetto. Per Rudling, the Diadia Vasia was formed in September 1942 by combining two brigades. By March 1943, the brigade contained three companies that totaled over 300 fighters (Rudling 2012, 35). Kaganovitsh also mentions Aleksandrovitsh and his partisan group in volume one of this same text (Kaganovitsh Vol. 1 1956, 378). Smolar says of the Diadia Vasia commander: "He was the first partisan commander (his name was Voromanski) who had held out his hand to us in those most difficult days" (TMG 1989, 154).

Aleksandrovitsh is also mentioned multiple times in four of Smolar's books: Fun minsker geto, Sovetishe yidn hinter geto-tsoymen, Vu bistu, Khaver Sidorov?, and The Minsk Ghetto. As central figures in the ghetto underground, Smolar and Aleksandrovitsh worked closely together to take Jews from the ghetto to the partisans. Smolar writes, "Khayim Aleksandrovitsh, with his cold-bloodedness and his immense political experience, was absolutely necessary while figuring out the fundamental questions of our underground work" (FMG 1946, 135-136).

Smolar also recounts that "I had warned Alesandrovitsh to get his wife Mashe and their young daughter Noimele away from the ghetto immediately. On March 2 [1942] she went out with one of the 'labor brigades'—and never returned. Haim demanded that we send him into the forest to fight with the partisans" (TMG 1989, 74).

Fogel's online Yiddish Leksikon tells that Aleksandrovitsh's wife was murdered during the March 2nd Purim Aktsye (Aktion) and that his daughter was buried alive, possibly a reference to yet one more inconceivably sadistic event that took place during that terrible time. As Smolar describes, during the Purim Aktsye, the Nazi governor Kommissar Wilhelm Kube, accompanied by Einsatzcommando leader Adolf Eichmann, had his squads lead the children from the ghetto orphanage to a freshly dug pit on Ratomski Street: "At his signal the murderers began throwing the children into the ditch and covering them with sand. The screams and cries could be heard far into the ghetto. Children stretched out their hands, pleading for their lives. Kommissar Kube walked alongside the ditch, tossing pieces of candy into it" (TMG 1989, 73).

In his 1979 interview with Claude Lanzmann in Israel, Smolar told how, as Kube threw sweets at them, the children cried "Feter, shit undz nisht keyn zamd in di oygn!" ("Uncle, don't throw sand in our eyes!").

Aleksandrovitsh apparently survived the war. Smolar tells of seeing him in the march of 30,000 partisans held in Moscow on 16 July 1944: "It was Haim Aleksandrovitsh, marching by the side of "Diadia Vasya" (Voromanski), pioneer of the partisan movement and my good friend from the Minsk ghetto" (TMG 1989, 151). Fogel notes that "After the victory over Hitler, he was awarded high decorations. According to published notices, after the war he was partially paralyzed and was placed in a hospital in Minsk."

Enemies

Usually, when "the German" returned to our cave we would cluster around him, and although he was always dead tired, we would not leave him alone until he had laid out for us everything he had accomplished while he was away. He was a scout, and his specialty was mainly "cleaning out" the area of local enemies. In this he would demonstrate such feats that the most skillfully disguised enemy would be forced to show his hand. "The German" possessed such a nose that he would, as he himself loved to boast, "sniff out their carcasses up to a mile away."

He was the only one that, contrary to orders, had the right to wear an exclusively German uniform. (According to the command, something from the clothing had to testify that the wearer was a partisan and not a German.) It was probably for this reason that we called him "the German," although his appearance bore immediate witness that he was far from being an Aryan. He also spoke German, even though it was interlaced with Yiddish words.

This time, when "the German" descended into the cave, he did not as usual approach the small burning stove. The group noticed that something had happened, so they didn't bother him, but made a place for him in the sleeping area so that he could stretch out.

At night we went out on a combat mission to blow up a bridge. When we came back the next morning, we found "the German"—to the astonishment of us all—lying just as we had left him. Our noisy recounting of all our "seven strokes of good luck" while doing away with the bridge and its guards, didn't move him at all. He remained lying there with open eyes, as if the entire matter was of no concern to him.

The story of "the German" began to greatly intrigue all of us. What in the world had happened to him? Quietly, we sent out a member of our unit in order to report to the squad commander about the sudden "melancholy" of the scout. That person returned quickly with a terrified look, informing us with a shrug of his shoulders that he had ... learned nothing. "The only thing is," he quietly informed us, "the commander cursed fiercely; he said, 'Let him lie there and suffer, if it doesn't lift him up out of his place.'"

The group could rest no longer. We began to make inquiries to comrades in intelligence—perhaps they knew something. Maybe those who had stayed on the base while we were off on our operation had some information? Nothing of the sort, no one knew a thing.

In the afternoon, the command was suddenly issued to harness the horses and sleighs, and to quickly begin taking everything out of the camp that could be transported. It was clear: we were "pulling out," we were changing our base. But what had happened? No one, not even those in intelligence, had heard that the enemy had appeared anywhere close.

When it became dark, we abandoned the base. Alongside us, heavily dragging his feet, was the silent "German." We surmised that our rapid departure from our base was related to "the German's" silence. This lay heavily on everyone's heart. We were leaving a warm, familiar place surrounded by peasants we knew. Now, wherever we might end up, there awaited us only deep snow and frozen pines that offered little protection against the wind. Of course it wasn't the first time, but the agitation had never been so strong as it was now—due solely to the suspicion that it was the fault of one of our own, and moreover, one that was considered to be among the best, the most agile ....

"The German," as if sensing the accumulation of ill will towards him, began turning his head to all sides, looking for someone. He moved in closer to our group and began to keep pace with our steps. No one drew him into conversation; he himself began to present his case. And although throughout his entire narrative there was no hint of defending himself—on the contrary, he repeated several times, "It's my fault, mine alone!"—one nevertheless sensed that from us, his old fighting companions, he expected a little compassion, at least a word of consolation....

"...I was informed that two women had gotten off the highway onto a distant country road. No one described to me any type of identifying marks. The only thing said, was that they were surely female partisans. Their clothing testified to this. And precisely this seemed suspicious to me. Coming from the main road, they certainly should have been dressed in civilian town clothing, especially our women.

"I sent out some of my scouts, and we kept the two women under observation. Without stopping them anywhere, we determined that they were walking in the direction of our base. Who were they? Where were they coming from, and who had given them such a precise route to follow?

"It occurred to me to submit the women to a brief examination, before they were stopped by our perimeter guard. I had two of my scouts change into German clothing, and the three of us hid in the nearest hamlet. When on the road, which was a few hundred meters from the hamlet, there appeared two silhouettes, I sent out my scouts on horseback, instructing them not to utter a single word—except for a menacing "H-A-L-T," and to bring the two women here to me. I managed to prepare the householders of the hamlet—above all, that they should put on a deathly-frightened face.

"Before me stood two fully molded female partisans. One was dark and good-looking, wearing boots and pants, with a short leather jacket on top. The other, who was older, wore a small fur coat girded with a leather belt. The younger one showed not a trace of fear as she stood before me—an officer of the German army. She spoke a little German, and responded freely to my questions. The older one stood there, flustered. Looking around on all sides, she edged up closer to the younger one, as if she wanted to protect herself from everything around.

"'In the forest on a stroll, is that not so, my beauties?

"'...Oh, the woods are nice, the birdsong is especially beautiful... there are different birds in the forest... which of these do the young ladies like the best; aren't they the ones that go pow-pow?'

"The older one became deathly pale. The younger smiled and stood there, perplexed. At the same time, I flew into a fury and threw every German curse I knew at the owners of the hamlet, driving them out of the hut. I politely requested the girls to lay their weapons on the table, if they possessed any. The younger one immediately pulled from her pocket a small French pistol, and laid it on the table. The older one glanced back behind her, caught sight of the stern gaze of my two scouts, and began to pull out from under her coat a Nagan revolver.

"I saw that there wouldn't be an opportunity to have a long discussion. But I was not yet sufficiently sure who actually had sent them here.

"'The road was difficult? Surely you lost your way?'

"The younger one with a light coquettishness answered, 'It doesn't matter, we're used to walking on foot.'

"Well, you were instructed precisely how to go . . . .'

"The younger one wanted to respond with something. Suddenly she pulled herself back and cast a quick glance in the direction of the older one. Being met with her tense, piercing eyes, she replied:

"'Yes, we know the way . . . .'

"Suddenly the older one came up close to me so quickly that my scouts swayed from their place. Quietly, but emphasizing every word, she informed me with reproach in her voice:

"'Herr Officer, you should not detain us. In any case, you must take these peasants, the live witnesses, away from here immediately, otherwise we can go no farther. I think that you have understood me.'

"I no longer had any doubts whom I had before me. However, I had to seize the thread and pursue it further.

"'Now you can't go any farther. You'll run straight into my soldiers again, and your release will become known in the forest. We must wait a bit.'

"'That's fine,' the younger one seized the idea. 'We will go back to Station 1, and we'll wait there.'

"'In the city then?' I questioned her further, not betraying my fear that the taut thread would snap.

"'No, Station 1 is now in our village.'

"'Oh, wonderful. We'll go there, to the village. As for the peasants, these are my people, so tomorrow you will be here again.'

"We set out in the sleigh, and my scouts understood without any order being given that they must drive along the same road on which the 'young ladies' had walked towards us. We bundled the women in furs, ostensibly so that no one on the road would recognize them. Not far from the highway, not knowing which way to continue, I turned to the ladies: perhaps one of them would like to take the reins. The younger one took them gladly, cast a glance around and instructed us to travel back, and at the first path to turn to the left.

"This gave me a blow to the heart. This was, after all, the very village where all our saboteurs stopped before they went across the highway to the railroad line. Here, in this village, was where I had my own team . . . .

"I had not yet managed to think this terrible thought to its conclusion when our sled suddenly stopped. My feet felt like they'd been paralyzed, and I could barely drag them down onto the ground. The girls walked, as if towards their own home, to the hut which I had, for months long, regarded as my official residence . . . .

"I didn't recognize my own voice when I ordered the mistress of the hut to call her husband. The astonished faces of the women when they heard me speak in a language other than German, slightly restored my equilibrium. The village elder or "starosta" (as we would call him), met me with his usual broad, welcoming smile, which immediately melted into a grimace over his now-pale face. He had spotted the "young ladies."

"This had never yet happened to me, but this time it did happen, and it was my own fault. I didn't allow the starosta to utter a word. I pounced on him with my pistol. I felt nothing except my boiling blood that burned my insides, rose up into my throat, pounded inside my head, and flooded my eyes. By the time I heard right next to my ear the whisper of my scout: 'Commander, calm down,' I lay in complete impotence on the bench. Only now did the wails of the starosta's wife reach me. I caught sight of how the second scout had pinned the hands of the older 'female partisan' behind her back who, biting her lips, tried to tear herself away from him. The younger one, with her mouth open as if she couldn't catch her breath, lay frozen stiff leaning up against the chest of drawers.

"I actually understood right there on the spot what my mistake was, and as if trying to undo it, I ordered the starosta to be dragged up onto the sleigh. My lads, however, had already thrown a mere corpse onto it. So I again fell into despair, again grabbed my Nagan, and as if wanting to numb myself, emptied the entire cartridge of bullets. Only then did I fully recover. On a piece of white canvas, I wrote with a trembling hand, 'Thus we will do to all our enemies,' and ordered that the corpses be brought to the main road. There we tossed them out onto the very center, pinning to them the canvas with the inscription.

"By the time I came to the base, I was completely clear-headed. I reported to the commander: this is what happened; order that I be arrested. And he—instead of berating me as was his custom—began with ferocious coldness to spell out for me everything of which I was guilty: that I entrusted an agent of the enemy to spy for us, and this along the main road, so he 'spied' in such a way that he found out precisely where our base was—this was number one. That instead of bringing him in alive so that we could interrogate him, I put him in the ground a mute corpse—this was number two. That instead of bringing the 'young ladies' to us and through them pulling the thread even tauter, I had snapped it at the very beginning—that was point number three. Three crimes, for which I deserve three times three grams of lead. Is that clear?! And he immediately ordered me to go to the cave and catch up on sleep...."

* *
*

Fatigued, we dragged our feet through the deep snow. Our joints hurt. Drops of sweat poured out from under our winter hats. The day began to dawn in the east, and we caught sight of the contours of a dense forest. All of a sudden it became easier for us to pull the load of our own bodies. It also seemed that the dejected face of our "German" had become brighter; after unburdening himself, he surely had become easier at heart.

The Judgment

The verdict was extremely terse, with no sort of explanation: "The female partisan, Rive Yokhes, is being transferred from the household command to the sabotage group." And that was it, that was all.

In the detachment, the name Rive Yokhes was actually heard for the first time when the commander read out the verdict. For months, a middle-aged woman had bustled about the kitchen; no one knew who she was or where she came from. They had grown accustomed, whenever they descended into the valley—on the eve of setting out on a night mission, or at dawn after wearily dragging themselves back to camp from distant, dangerous roads—to seeing "the Mute" (thus they called her among themselves) at her place in the kitchen, always busy with scraping, cleaning, cooking.

In other circumstances, her name would have made a bit of an impression: What, she was Jewish! The dull worn-out weariness of her wrinkled face had rather suggested a life of hard service in a nobleman's manor, where Jewish maids were not hired. It would also have made an impression when the commander announced that the only woman in the squad would no longer be in the kitchen, but that men would from that day on peel potatoes, cook dinner, and do the laundry.

But now no one was surprised by it. No one even had any complaints when the always-tasty evening meal was this time disgusting, and also did not suffice for everybody. What had happened took away everyone's appetite. Quietly the men dispersed, each to wherever he had to be.

The next evening, when the sabotage group set out from the base, the commander, along with his adjutant Fedke, accompanied her up to the watch-point, quietly shook everyone's hand, and only to Rive tossed out a few words:

"What the commissar said was right . . . do as he commanded!"

* *
*

It probably would have ended as it always did: each one of the three prisoners in turn would have caught a bullet, and that would have been that. Maybe the partisans would also have had a little fun with them, so great was their resentment. On none of the captured Germans did they find a single bullet. Even the pistols were empty. It was clear: they had shot until the very end and surrendered only when they had no alternative. And here, before the staff, each one of them maintained that they were just little lambs. In sum, they themselves wanted to surrender; they were fed up with the war. And the main thing—"Hitler kaput."

The crowd was indignant. What sons of whores! Maybe we should go bring them a pork chop and clap them on the back, these brave lads—as if the killing of one of our best saboteurs today had nothing whatever to do with them.

Nevertheless, the group stood with dignity and listened attentively to the commissar's patient, almost courteous inquiry. Only to his translations did the group react with wisecracks and double-edged blessings, which evidently made the Germans uneasy. They would surely have stood there trading witticisms until the usual verdict came, and as usual someone would have announced "Here, I'm ready to help," so as to put an end to the matter. But then something occurred that left the whole group, including the staff, dumbfounded.

No one heard or noticed that "the Mute" had sidled up to the gathering around the command post. Suddenly they heard a ragged, spasmodic bellowing and a muffled sound of vigorous blows. Only when one of the Germans, with a murderous ferocity, started running forward in a zigzag, was he stopped by a short blast of automatic weapons fire, and the crowd tore itself from its spot. Someone threw himself at the tangle on the ground and by force dragged away "the Mute," who stubbornly refused to break her grip, clamped to the body of the German. Only then did the men notice her strangely altered face. Her smoldering eyes looked at everyone insolently, and a fiery redness appeared on her pale face, driving away every trace of its usual dullness.

"Under guard!" gasped out the commander. Partisans threw themselves at the only surviving German.

"I mean her!" The commander pointed a finger at Rive—and already somewhat calmed, added:

"A trial is a trial! Let no one interfere where it's not needed."

* * *

Afterwards the guard told what had happened, and people knew at once that it was true:

"The Mute" was as talkative as ten orators. When the guard entered the arrest-cave that night, at first he didn't hear the commissar say a single word. Only Rive spoke. And she spoke as if she were not the one that needed to be tried, but he, the commissar.

Thus did the group find out exactly how Rive came to the forest, carrying in her arms her only child, who had been shot dead. It was her tiny child who had taken the bullet that the "resettlement" men shot at Rive as she escaped the ghetto. And after that they learned of Rive's trek through woods and villages with the dead child in her arms and with a furious, roiling heart, a walk that led her through deadly perils all the way there to the base. And here, her resentment grew: a cook, they'd ordered her to be, a washerwoman! So she had worked, toiled—to spite herself. But now it ends! Enough! Let them put her on trial....

And this is what the guard overheard: a curt injunction from the commissar, which could have been both a judgment and a command, and what he said to her was this:

"You will go and you will pass judgment!"

Historical Notes: *Smolar describes a story almost identical to this one in an undated personal interview. One night when he was the duty officer, a guard reported that there was a woman crouched under a tree, insisting* on seeing the commander. He had her brought before him and she told him that she'd run away from the ghetto "after seeing a German split her child's head in two. Now all she wanted was to inflict pain on the Germans. She was ready to do anything. She had to avenge the death of her baby" (Tec 2003, 330).

The woman requested that she take part in all anti-German missions, but she was instead placed on kitchen duty. She carried out her assignments but resentful, refused to speak, earning the nickname "The Mute One."

One day five German prisoners were brought into the base, including a high-ranking officer. Smolar, fluent in German, handled the interrogation. As the five prisoners with their hands bound stood before him, he spotted the woman approaching them. He didn't think too much of it, but "in a split second, I saw the woman jump with a knife in hand. She pushed the knife into the back of the highest-ranking officer. He fell instantly and never moved. First came shock, then the horrible knowledge that our most important catch was gone."

Smolar intervened to prevent her from being executed; the commandant instead ordered that she be sent on "the worst, most dangerous military operations . . . Let her discover what it really means to fight!" This punishment, however, was transformative for the woman. Adapting immediately to military life, she performed excellently in mission after mission. She obtained a reputation as a heroic soldier, and survived the war with military distinctions. Unfortunately, Smolar never provides her name (Tec 2003, 332).

The Czech Rifle

The Czech rifle was to blame for everything. How much did Tsilye Botvinik exhaust herself before she managed to steal that rifle from the German armament workshops? How many terrifying close calls did she survive as she smuggled the rifle past the Hitlerist control points, past the sentries at the ghetto gates, and afterwards—all the way until she reached the partisan detachment! And when she had finally made it to the detachment, the painful ordeal of the owner of the Skoda-rifle had not yet ended. Scores of interested parties coveted the rifle. Truth be told, this was a fine instrument, and Tsilye had also brought a considerable quantity of bullets with her—and here there were quite a few partisans who were weaponless. They began arguing with Tsilye: "Your place is to occupy yourself with woman's work. There's a world of work to do: cook the meals, do the laundry, care for the sick. Give the rifle over to us men. We will defeat the Hitlerist swine with it." But Tsilye held her ground: No and no! She hadn't safeguarded the rifle and with it traversed a hundred and fifty kilometers, just to be in the kitchen, but rather in order to shoot with it. The matter even reached the detachment commander.

Tsilye stood by her claim that this brand-new Czech rifle must stay with her. She became part of the diversionary unit in the demolition group of Lieutenant Aron Shmushkevitsh.

In order to reach the most heavily guarded positions of the Hitlerist transport, in addition to audacity you also need a lot of skill, and more than that—tenacity. After all, it's a matter of meeting the enemy at one of his most sensitive locations....

For the first diversionary act, the group chose the railway line that ran right by a large freight station. Until then there had been no diversionary acts carried out in this place.

Tsilye goes to scout out the surrounding area. Spotlights illuminate the entire terrain. The Hitlerists are on the alert. But not so much as to notice a small group of partisans silently sneaking in. Aron lays the explosives. Tsilye helps him. She lays her body right across the rails and picks up the slightest rustle with her ear. It seems they will be lucky. The scarcely audible tremor that goes through the rails is a portent that something is already moving along them. It still takes a long time until the labored chugging of a locomotive can be heard in the distance. It's a sign: a heavily laden adversary is on its way.

And so it was. Secure and carefree (since there are no woods here) the heavy transport approached the railway station. But it never arrived. The locomotive, along with twenty-two railroad cars of live and inanimate cargo, were crushed together into one great heap. Train traffic along this railroad sector was blocked for an entire forty-eight hours. In wartime, this was significant.

The commander of the division goes around very anxious: according to the division's capabilities, over the course of a month such and such a number of the enemy's trucks should have been destroyed, and here, as if out of spite, it's not happening! When Tsilye set off with her diversionary group to the railway station Zielone to mine the tracks, she carried in her heart this wish: that railroad cars carrying trucks should run over the mine. The wish remained just a wish: a troop train filled with live Hitler youth set it off. Too bad, but this too was partisan bread and butter.

Just a month later, after they'd set off the third explosion, twelve platforms of German trucks, fresh from the factory, were left lying at the Krizshovke railroad station.

Partisan demolition teams know this well: you crawl out of your own skin, dodge the cunning obstacles that lie in your path, trenches, ambush-points, enclosures, mines; you make it to the train and— nothing! It's not working!

The anniversary of the great Socialist October Revolution approaches. There's a partisan tradition: On that day, let it resound! Five times Tsilye's group tried to go up to the detonation objective. True, they'd picked a pretty dangerous spot: between a railroad bridge and a spotlight projection point. They'd already managed to lay the TNT, and suddenly, as if out of nowhere, "Halt!" Tsilye kept a cool head. She succeeded in recovering the TNT (the most precious item for a partisan minelayer): rockets were flying, and the surroundings were lit up bright as day. Automatic weapons and machine guns hammered the entire area with tracer bullets. The partisan group left that hell without a loss. What next? They were adamant: they would not return to camp. You don't come back empty-handed!

The group lurked for a long time by the railway line, and it was not until five days after the holiday that they succeeded in getting the job done. Indeed, it was after a delay, yet with a calm and clear conscience, that they reported to the commander: Succeeded in annihilating a troop transport of twenty-seven railroad cars filled with fascist front-line thugs, who owing to their "special service" were going on leave to Germany. The partisan group gave them an endless furlough . . . .

Certainly, cooking a meal was a very important thing for partisans, and washing out a shirt was simply an obligation of comradeship; Tsilye Botvinik would have done it gladly in her every free moment, with a whole heart. But to finish off five of the enemy's troop trains was also something, especially for a woman who, while in the ghetto underground, had dreamt of that moment when she could, with her new Czech rifle, shoot bullets into the hearts of the murderers who had slaughtered her entire family.

Historical Notes: *Tsilye served as both a scout and a demolition expert in the Kutuzov otriad, part of the Jewish Frunze Detachment. She also brought Jews out of the ghetto and into the forest (Kaganovitsh Vol 2., 234).*

Tsilye's full story is told in the Russian book Moving Through the Years Gone By, later translated into English. When the Minsk ghetto was established in July 1941, Tsilye was married and struggling with a difficult pregnancy. Her husband, Lev Dreizin, a lieutenant in the Russian Army, was fighting along with her brother Zakhar at the front. She and family tried to evacuate, but were turned back by the Germans. Her daughter was born in November in the ghetto, but due to the horrific conditions there, Tsilye was in no shape to care for a newborn. Unable to feed her newborn daughter in the ghetto, in desperation she gave her over to a Russian woman, Zaytseva.

די פּאַרטיזאַנערן צילע באָטווינִיק,
וועלכע האָט אויפגעריסן פינף דייטשישע
עשעלאָנען.

**"The partisan Tsilye Botvinik,
who blew up five German troop trains."** (FMG 1946, 140)

Her contact for Zaytseva was killed during an aktion in July 1942. After the war, Tsilye was unable to find the Zaytseva family or her daughter: "I spent many years looking for my girl but in vain. I never found out what happened to her..." (Guy 2016, 14)

Tsilye, longtime friend of ghetto underground leader Misha Gebelev, joined the ghetto underground and worked in a German munitions workshop along with another underground member, Katya Tsirlin. Their job was to clean and lubricate the weapons. "From the very outset, Katya and I decided that we would do whatever we could to damage the firearms," she later wrote (Guy, 38). They also smuggled out disassembled rifle parts. In the summer of 1943, Smolar (now a partisan in the Starostelsky Forest), sent a guide to bring her and others out of the ghetto. They were instructed to bring all their weapons and medical supplies with them, including the Czech rifle of the story: "I carried my Czech carbine, which I assembled from the parts I took from the German munitions shop" (Guy, 100).

Although she was able to keep her rifle, Tsilye's time with the partisans was difficult. While standing guard with the Kutuzov Detachment and unaware of a password change, she mistakenly challenged a reconnaissance unit. For this she was badly beaten and ultimately removed from the unit. She also had a confrontation when she was sent to Sholem Zorin's brigade on assignment from her unit. Zorin, short of weapons for his own fighters, attempted to take her rifle. She refused, it was taken by force, and she was arrested and held under a fir tree for three days without food. When Smolar learned of her arrest, he was able to set her free. She then joined Tuvia Bielski's detachment, where she received better treatment.

Both she and her brother survived the war. Tsilye returned to Minsk after the war, remarried, and had two sons who became physicians. Her husband, Avsey Lupyan, passed away in 1983; in 1990 she and her family emigrated to the United States. Tsilye lived in Brooklyn, New York and died in 2015 at the age of 98.

The President of Our Capital

Had it been anyone else, he certainly would have fared badly. Tevl got off with only a mocking remark at his expense from the brigade commissar Sobtshik, and with a dozen disparaging looks from other members of the staff. With a feigned sheepish smile, Tevl gave the appearance of acquiescing in this treatment, swallowed, and remained sitting wordlessly on the small stool in the far corner of the packed, smoky peasant hut.

Of course, it never would have occurred to Tevl, the adjutant of brigade commander Vasilevski, to intervene uninvited in the tense conversation on the eve of the big battle. He knew his duties well: to understand commands without having them spelled out, to carry them out, and to report back quickly, "These are the facts, Comrade Colonel!" Even now he certainly wouldn't have dared open his mouth, except that it concerned the execution of a plan that he, Tevl, had already presented dozens of times in every detail to the colonel, when the latter was in a cheerful mood and would strike up with Tevl one of their never-ending nighttime conversations.

Tevl had grown fond of the brigade commander. For the first time in his thirty-odd years of life, he had met a person not of his own people to whom he, Tevl, could become attached without reservation, and to forget entirely that between the two of them there stood on one side long years of yeshiva learning and the Besmedresh environment, and on the other twenty-five years of professional military service, first as a simple soldier in the Tsar's army and now as a partisan brigade commander. Vasilevski was well acquainted with Tevl's past. The partisans who hailed from the area had told him about it in every detail—of Tevl's ordination as a rabbi and of Tevl's prestige even among the local peasants, who would come to him to settle disputes. Why the colonel had settled on him as his assistant, Tevl didn't know. In the beginning it had terrified him—how would he do his job, given that he had no inkling of worldly things, not to speak of military matters? He wasn't so much afraid of the potential anger of the commander as he was of ridicule by the partisans—trained military men, many of whom would have been happy to be the brigade commander's adjutant. "May this ridicule, God forbid, not extend to the other Jews," worried Tevl, and this worry kept him welded to the colonel, not taking a step away from him. And just as if to spite him, the commander gave no sign that he noticed him—Tevl had no assignments whatsoever from him. It was only late at night, when all commands for that twenty-four-hour period had been issued, all reports listened to, and all liaison officers sent out with missions to the detachments, that the colonel would engage in a long conversation with his adjutant.

A descendant of a Polish family exiled to Siberia, Vasilevski had inherited the trait of those freedom fighters, convicts sentenced to hard labor: getting to the bottom of problems that were in complete contrast to their very simple surroundings. And when Vasilevski launched into his beloved talk about how the present day would not be worth spilling a single drop of sweat—let alone blood—unless there were sown in it the seeds of an exalted tomorrow, Tevl sensed in the colonel a kinship with his own soul, which in its striving for completion had compelled him to decline a position as a rabbi, lest he become a "professional." And although it was in a foreign, poorly-mastered language, Tevl without hesitation laid out before this idealistic man—the very one who just an hour earlier had given out one command after another: to shoot, to lay waste, to smash—his, Tevl's, own vision of the moment, in which one must immediately compensate, heal, console, and above all rescue.

In his great zeal, Tevl failed to notice the angry slanting wrinkles knotting the colonel's forehead. At that moment, the military man rebelled against the insolence of this ignoramus, who permitted himself to question the worth of our armed struggle. But he didn't interrupt him, and Tevl argued his point:

"You yourself surely know as well as I: a single regular army company at the front kills in one day more of the enemy's troops than do all of us here in the forest in the course of months. Consequently, combat is not our essential purpose. Our strength is a higher one. We smash the blind faith in the enemy's omnipotence, even where he is in fact omnipotent. We lay down our morals and our laws, we strike fear into the alien ruler and allow him no authority over us. We carry with us the belief in our superiority, and the person of faith responds, as in all times, by glorifying in his legends our invincible power, and these very legends serve, serve, as the best of weapons...."

During one such passionate evening conversation, Tevl cautiously posed a question to the colonel: what did he think about the possibility of crushing the German garrison in the town R.?

"We do many operations, and they are scattered throughout different corners of the region. This is all well and good. But the really effective move, one that would convince everyone of our strength, would be if we tackled an assignment of this kind."

As usual, Tevl spoke long and heatedly, and demonstrated that the garrison at R. blocked their access to the east, that their saboteurs must go miles out of their way in order to break through to those essential railroad lines—again irritating the colonel that the "Rabiner" (as the partisans called Tevl behind his back) should explain to him, the military man, the strategic importance of the town R. By then, Vasilevski was ready to put an end to the conversation and show his adjutant that there were boundaries he should not cross, but Tevl was not yet done and would not allow himself to be interrupted.

"I cannot," said he, "I can't keep to myself any unexpressed thoughts. Yes, commander, it is my hometown. And there, in the ghetto, remain people who expect from me, from us, retribution, consolation, salvation...."

Days passed, and Tevl watched how his deepest desire began to take the shape of a precisely-worked out battle plan. Several times he accompanied the brigade commander to several detachments where mock battles were being carried out. Tevl was already well-versed in all the details of the plan. He saw mistakes being made in rehearsals of the battle. During the day, however, he was only the adjutant and stood in a disciplined silence at the service of the colonel. Only at night did he share with his friend Vasilevski his observations and suggested corrections; the colonel did not even notice the vanishing of his previous resentment when Tevl would make a comment about his, the commander's, military matters.

It was also during the final deliberations in the peasant hut located halfway to the town R., that Tevl, uninvited, interjected his observation that the plan lacked the most important thing (that it would succeed, of that Tevl had no doubt). "What's lacking is how to control the situation after expelling the Germans." The colonel received his words just as he did during the frequent evening talks. But the commissar unexpectedly knocked him back on his stool with his derisive response:

"Then we'll appoint you as city president."

And two dozen pairs of eyes of the squad commanders pierced him with their mocking glare. Deflated, Tevl sat there and didn't even hear the colonel's argument that "In all seriousness, we must plan for this," that "until now we've never controlled any cities, and it's not just a matter of smashing the garrison . . . ."

Tevl didn't even clearly catch the last command that the colonel read out to the commanders of all battle sectors, in which his name was also mentioned. A final handshake from the commander, and only then did he grasp it: in the order issued before the entire brigade, he, Tevl Shimanovitsh, Colonel Vasilevski's adjutant, was appointed military commandant of the liberated town R.

* * *

On the high shore of the town's quiet river lay piled up a mound, and upon it a plaque with an inscription:
Here lies the heroic partisan
Tevl Shimanovitsh
Who perished in the battle for the liberation of his hometown.

Many times, the Germans tried to take back the town R., which still lay far from the forward positions of the front. Often, they would succeed in re-occupying it, sometimes even for a lengthy period. But even then, the town was called by everyone in the region nothing but "the Partisan Capital." As soon as the Germans were driven out, partisan detachments would come, leave, and come back again – day and night—settle in ordinary dwellings, go visit the city's populace, and from there disperse across the entire province in order to carry out battle operations and bring back with them the latest news of victories and losses.

And every single partisan group would regard it as its duty, before all else, to pay a visit to the "President of the Capital."

Historical Notes: *The antisemitism of other partisan groups was a grave issue for Jewish partisans and those escaping the ghettos and trying to reach the partisans; many Jews were robbed of their weapons when they encountered these groups, and usually killed. Accusations of Jews as spies and saboteurs were also common. Smolar recounts how while at staff headquarters, Tevl Shimanovitsh, the adjunct to Major Vasilievitsh, came galloping up on a horse to report the murder of several Jewish women who, having just cross the Niemen River, lay dead on the shore, slain by other partisans: "These Jewish women had been murdered by our own 'friends'—by other partisans" (TMG 1989, 127-128). Both Smolar and Tevl were overwhelmed with grief and fury over yet another senseless act, this time on supposedly friendly territory. Smolar describes the scene: "They were dead. It was obvious that these women had tried to save themselves. They had succeeded in swimming through Niemen and then they were murdered. They had come to our side. On our side there were no Germans. We stood there stunned" (Tec 1993, 155).*

Returning to headquarters, Smolar was met by Vladimir Tsaryuk, official representative of the Belarussian partisans. Asking who had murdered these women, Smolar describes how, speaking softly and not making eye contact, Tsaryuk "explained": "We were warned by reliable sources that the Gestapo had sent out a group of women to put poison in our food kettles—we're in a war—can't do anything about it now ..." (TMG, 128)

Smolar remembers Tevl with fondness: "We all loved Tevl Shimanovitsh, who had once been a yeshiva student and even been ordained as a rabbi." Smolar also tells how Major Vasilievitsh, commander of the Zhukov brigade, did indeed hold him in high regard and consulted him on military questions, especially those dealing with the terrain that Tevl was intimately familiar with.

Old Shimen Tells a Tale....

Usually when the partisan campfire is burning the mood becomes milder. People seat themselves around it, pressed closely one against the other, and look on with wonder at how pleasant is the hissing of a green pine twig when tossed on the fire. From time to time, almost mechanically, a hand will throw on a dry branch, a dug-up stump. Often no one wants to budge from the spot. Their eyes are half-closed. Then begin the favorite moments of the short partisan rest break. The acknowledged storyteller begins his "Once there was ...."

The campfire had blazed up quite lively, but none of the group of ghetto Jews who had arrived in Kolodin Forest had any desire whatsoever to sit around it. Tensions were at a high level—they had just tossed their yellow stars into the fire, they'd just listened to the harsh talk of Commander Yisroyl Lapidus, who had explained the law of ruthless battle and boundless revenge. Each of them knew: the way back was cut off forever. Yet there, in the ghetto, Leyzer Losik's mother and little sister remained behind. Someone had left a father, another a mother, a wife, brothers, sisters—how is it going to turn out?

Yisroyl Lapidus says: Let us arm ourselves well, let us take on the fight that we came here for—then we'll succeed in bringing out scores and hundreds of our brothers and sisters.

Their hearts feel lighter, they sit down by the fire, and one of the oldest of the group—Shimen Lapidus—begins his tale about how it once was, twenty-some years ago, when he, Shimen, went off for the first time to fight as a partisan in the White Russian woods.

"... the young Soviet country was besieged from all sides—it was the difficult year of battle, 1919. We see the enemy, but he—he doesn't see us. We caused him so much suffering that he was careful not to show up again in our territory. Now it will once again be this way. You have only to keep your ears and eyes always on the alert, and the bullet in your rifle clean and dry. Here, for instance . . . ."

The lads perk up their ears, so as to hear Shimen's tale. But this time they didn't get to hear him out. Instead, they saw him, saw him clearly, with their own eyes . . . .

The order came from the commander: Be ready to fight!

Sixty men, armed with rifles and four machine guns, set off for the main thoroughfare that goes from Pukhovitshi to Starye Dorogi. They hid themselves by the village of Omelne, camouflaged and patiently ("Patience is the key!" says the seasoned old partisan, Shimen) waited . . . and their patience was rewarded.

Nine freight trucks bearing Gestapo men, armed from head to toe, traveled down the highway to carry out their usual daily bloody work in the surrounding rebellious villages. So they drove and drove and . . . didn't reach their destination.

"Fire!" ordered Commander Yisroyl Lapidus. After the first blast, the bewildered fascists began pouring out of the vehicles. Curses and groans echoed all around. The partisans closed in, and a struggle began, one on one. Avrom Kholyavski splits open the skull of a blonde brute, and Yoysef Yankelevitsh chokes a second one with his bare hands. Old Shimen is already on top of a German truck, and calls out:

"Slaughter them, dear brothers! Remind them how it was in the ghetto!"

Seventy-four Hitler-bandits were laid out like logs on the highway. Not all of them, though, had such "luck": eight had fallen alive into partisan hands. When these eight heard the partisans speaking Yiddish, their blood curdled, even before the bullet brought each the punishment he'd earned . . . .

The campfire blazes merrily in the provisional camp of the partisan detachment of ghetto Jews. Although the clothing of many of them is wet through and through, no one is drying himself out. They are so busy that they've forgotten everything. What can be sweeter than to tally up and carry the seized trophies of the enemy, the joy of a successful act of vengeance? The hope that with the captured weapons a hundred new partisans would be armed, reinvigorated their aching limbs. Forgotten was the respite earned after the intense battle operation. A rumor ran through the villages in the neighboring areas: The Jewish partisans have appeared, and are showing the killers what they're made of. They've already successfully done away with such and such a number of SS men. Yisroyl Lapidus' detachment, which came into being in the ghetto, began attracting people of different nationalities.

* * *

For partisans, this was a very difficult matter—to take on unexpectedly an open battle with the enemy. The Fifth (or, as it was called, Lapidus') Detachment heads to the railroad on a military assignment. Until it gets dark, they rest up in the village of Great Sentshi. Just then the intelligence report arrives: a heavily armed enemy unit is approaching—with cannons and machine guns. There is still enough time to retreat, but this is not the custom of Lapidus' people. They take on the uneven fight. The enemy fires rockets; they call for help from neighboring garrisons. Tanks arrive from Pukhovitshi. The partisans pull back to the nearby village, dig in there, and don't allow the very much larger and better-armed enemy to get through. After this fight, the detachment heads off to fulfill the carefully planned assigned task.

Once again the partisans sit by the campfire, and although they're tired, they listen closely to Old Shimen's story:

"Once there was . . . ."

Historical Notes: *Smolar tells of Shimen (Shimon) Lapidus, noting that although he was already old, he was able to keep up the pace with his son Israel's new partisan detachment. He was a vital member of the group, sharing stories of his experiences during the "difficult year of battle, 1919," most likely a reference to the Soviet westward offensive (1918-1919) of the Russian Civil War (1917-1923). He also taught the younger partisans how to survive in the forest (TMG, 154-155).*

Smolar recounts the same battle on the road between Pukhovitshi and Starye Dorogi, describing how "Old Shimon" jumped on a truck and, swinging his rifle butt, clubbed the Nazis on the head with it: "As if he were the Commander himself, he kept urging on the partisans: 'Pay them, youngsters, pay them back for the ghetto, for Tutshinka!'" (155). Tutshinka (Tuchinka) was an execution site outside the Minsk ghetto where on November 7, 1941, between 12,000 and 17,000 Jews were brought out in trucks and murdered (Epstein, 102-103).

In the memorial book Lebn un umkum fun Olshan (361), Yisroyl Lapidus is mentioned as a Jewish partisan commander in the Kolodin Forest who had shot a Jewish partisan, Mikhoyl (Mishke) Baranov from Minsk; another report tells that Lapidus ordered the execution of a Mishka Baran for stealing milk (Finkel, 171). Epstein (220) names Lapidus as the commissar of the Kutuzov brigade, also known as Detachment No. 5, or as Smolar calls it in this story, the "Fifth (or, as it was called, Lapidus') Detachment."

Smolar notes (FMG, 158) that Leyzer Losik, along with one other partisan, Avrom Khalitsvski, had each brought down 12 enemy troop transports, and were each awarded the silver partisan medal.

Smolar also reports that a peasant tasked by Leyzer Losik to bring Jews out of the Minsk ghetto did bring out Losik's mother and sister (FMG, 158). According to Cherney, Lapidus's parents and one son were killed in the first Aktion. When he led a group from the ghetto to form his partisan detachment in the woods, he walked at the head of the line with his wife and firstborn son (Porter 2021, 89-90).

The Password

The men loved him, the chief of intelligence, like life itself. He was a cheerful young man. Anecdotes, proverbs, parables—he had an endless supply of them. In every situation, whether in joy or in suffering, he was the one who would gather the group about him, entertain them, lift their spirits.

And yet they would start to tremble as soon as the intelligence chief summoned them to send them out on a mission. They trembled, not because of the difficulty of the task, nor the danger of being killed, but because of the chief's passwords. He didn't care much for the usual very plain partisan passwords. He would select such complicated ones that the lads would trudge along like sleepwalkers and practice them the whole way. He had a special fondness for poetic passwords. He would force them to learn by heart an entire stanza of Pushkin or Lermontov, first from top to bottom and then from bottom to top. Woe to him who couldn't grasp them quickly. The intelligence chief would wring him out like a wet rag.

Rakhmilke sat with the intelligence chief, listened attentively to his every word, till the roof of his mouth went dry from agitation. What would he do, given his weak command of Russian? How on earth would he memorize the password?

The task was a difficult one. The chief trusted him, his ability to manage it. Rakhmilke hailed from B., and it was reported that not far from there one of our raiding parties had airdropped. Someone needed to get there, make contact, and then use his own judgment as to what should be done. On the way he would need to stop in at two places where peasants lived—liaisons of the detachment—from whom he would receive more precise information.

And here the intelligence chief got to the most important

matter—the password! Rakhmilke began to stammer: he didn't know any Russian . . . he hadn't read Pushkin.

The chief fixed a pair of sympathetic eyes on him and, contrary to custom, began to impart to him the idea that life without poetry was colorless and impoverished. That one ought to know Pushkin. And in the middle of speaking he suddenly halted, as if something very important had occurred to him:

"Wait, you're a Jew, aren't you? Are you familiar with Sholem Aleichem?" And as if forgetting everything and everyone, the chief of intelligence began to rattle off the sayings of Tevye the Dairyman.

Although Rakhmilke didn't immediately manage to grasp the point of all the expressions in Russian, he would always burst out laughing, and the chief, laughing along with him, would straight away fire off a new one.

For the first time in all these years in the forest Rakhmilke felt, here in the intelligence chief's cave, the sharp longing for a familiar word. Under this influence, the verses that the commissar had drilled him in became more intimate.

When he left the forest along with his group, he no longer needed to repeat the difficult password. He remembered it easily. The words, although with an unusual newness, approached his mood.

* *
*

Rakhmilke did not find the liaison at home. When he wanted to set off into the field to seek him out, the peasant's wife stopped him and asked him not to go, so that outsiders wouldn't see him. It wasn't long before the liaison cautiously slipped into the hut. Measuring each word, Rakhmilke gave him the first phrase of the password. The peasant, not waiting until Rakhmilke finished the second phrase, anxiously reported that the police were searching in the neighborhood, and here, in his field, there was a girl.

"She is a 'female parachute raider'—so she says. She won't budge until I put her in touch with your group."

Rakhmilke hastily told the liaison to lead the way. His hand on his loaded pistol, he set out after him to the field. From the hay came sliding out a young, charming girl, whose dark eyes were wide open, more likely from wonder than fear. Rakhmilke ceased to feel the revolver in his hand. Simultaneously, he forgot his firm decision, made on the way there, that before anything else he would in the authoritative tone of a commander, demand the password from her. Instead of requesting it, he himself began to murmur:

"*Dika, petshalna, moltshaliva,*
Kak lan liesnaya boyazliva"[1]

The girl crawled completely out from the hay; with a broad smile on her face, she quietly fell into Rakhmilke's tone and began, like him, to whisper:

"*Ona, v'semye svoyeyi rodnoy*
Kazalas dievotshkoy tshuzhoy"[2]

She soon burst out in loud laughter:

"Do I really look to you like such a wild and frightened creature? What an encounter . . . with Pushkin . . . you're probably a poet?"

Only then did Rakhmilke realize that he had confounded one thing with another. Unnerved, he was barely able to utter:

"Password . . . I mean, you have to give the password . . . ."

"I know a lot of passwords. I need to get to you all quickly," and here the girl began hurriedly to brush the hay off of her dress, her hair, as if she was ready to go with him straight away. Rakhmilke pulled himself together. Before his eyes the image of the chief of intelligence loomed up. Rakhmilke sternly put a question to the girl:

"What do you mean by 'you all'? To the police?"

She slyly narrowed her eyes, focusing them sharply on Rakhmilke.

"I really mean to you . . . You serve in the police, don't you?"

Rakhmilke turned pale. Again, he felt the pistol in his pocket and stammering, began pelting her, half in Polish, half in Russian, with

---

1. *From Pushkin's "Yevgeniy Onyegin": "Wild, sad, silent, like a forest gazelle, frightened."*
2. *Pushkin: "In her own family, she seemed like a changeling girl."*

words from that partisan lexicon to be repeated only in the forest. He broke off suddenly when there reached his ears the quiet whispering of the gentle girlish voice:

"I too, am Jewish...."

Surprised, Rakhmilke gazed at her, as if only then did he notice her genuine Jewish eyes.

"Is that so... is that so..." he murmured.

Quickly he again recalled the chief's command: Trust no one, demand the password from everyone.

"Come with me," he ordered with feigned harshness. "We will see."

And as they set out for the path to the neighboring forest where the entire group of raiders should now be gathered, he repeated several times, as if he didn't have her in mind:

"Sholem Aleichem was a good writer, a good writer... do you remember any Sholem Aleichem? Our chief loves his quotes very much...."

Historical Notes: *The verse quoted in this story comes from Alexander Pushkin's* Yevgeny Onegin *(Eugene Onegin), a Russian novel written in verse and published serially between 1825 and 1832. The lines recited by Rakhmilke and the girl are from Chapter 2, Part 2, stanza 25.*

The Issue is Ready for Print

With Meyrim's bare foot in his hand, Vladek suddenly stood frozen in place. Meyrim himself, who had just then (as was usual in the early mornings) finished letting loose a string of the most bizarre multi-layered curses—on the pretext that the little bastard had not let him catch a few winks even for a moment—most unusually let his foot hang docilely in Vladek's hand. Meyrim's staring, fatigue-swollen eyes were fixed on the opening of our dirt cave. The ever-phlegmatic typesetter Lize, who after a night of working by the small kerosene lamp would be wholly deaf to everything around her—she too stood petrified, with the composing stick in her hand over an unfinished word.

In the narrow opening of our cave appeared the large head of curly black hair belonging to the commander of the explosives detachment, Dodye Potashnik.

Dodye's visits to our forest editorial office were not a novelty; scarcely would he return from a battle operation than he would immediately squeeze up to us in the cave wearing a wide grin, and with narrowed eyes station himself next to Lize and Vladek, peruse the proof sheets that lay before them, and marvel at how nimbly Lize pulled out each necessary letter from the font boxes. He would stand that way for a long time, humming the tune of some Rosh HaShone hymn, from which he would immediately break off when Meyrim began to help him via the quotation:

"The letters of the Law soar upward . . . ."

Dodye would then straighten up soldier-like, step back from the typeset "box" and before leaving, turn to me with his usual question:

"When will the 'poster' be ready?"

In Dodye's language a "poster" was what he called a newspaper, a front-line report, a call to arms to the population of the surrounding townships, a warning to the "Vlasov-ists"—all of the above, which he and his explosives detachment would take along with them, together with the TNT and bullets, when they set off on an operation against the enemy.

This would really get under Meyrim's skin: "A poster indeed! Such disdain for work of which the partisan general himself would say, 'You are doing holy work, my brothers; every letter—a stick of dynamite!'" He never missed the opportunity, did Meyrim, to reply with a sarcastic remark:

"Commander, people are saying you had a successful operation. You've done a good job undermining ... your own authority...."

This time Meyrim would certainly have forgiven Dodye, no matter what he answered, but Dodye lowered himself down onto the bottom bunk, scraped the ground with his heel, and was silent. Slowly, Meyrim slid down from his bed and quietly, not even washing up, stationed himself at the "box."

"Do you have anything to typeset, Editor?" he said to me.

"Lude will bring in the battlefront report soon. She wore herself out the entire night and couldn't pick anything up. The Krauts are causing trouble...."

Dodye began intensely listening in on our conversation. Slowly he came over to my improvised editor's desk and stiffly, imperiously interrupted:

"Write, Editor!

"... I've always argued with them: have patience, don't rush, don't get yourself all worked up, and they—as if it had nothing at all to do with them! It's my own fault—I didn't have to send Velfke, still a lad—a snot-nosed kid who'd never been under fire, and here ... Write, Editor!"

"Tell us, tell us how it came about."

Dodye stayed quiet for a few minutes, his long black eyelashes completely covering the pupils of his eyes. Three deep furrows lingered across his brow. We all sensed how hard it was for him to speak at this moment. So we too remained silent.

"Write, Editor." Dodye got up, began dragging his feet heavily across the cave and haltingly began to tell the story:

"From our Intelligence, we found out that two days ago a field cable had been laid at the third kilometer. Frankly, this was a job for 'musicians'[1] and I didn't even consider it an opportunity for us. Just then Velfke clings to me like glue and doesn't want to let it go: 'Send me, Commander. I'll creep through there like a cat.'

"At first I tried to shoo him away like an annoying fly. He didn't let it go, and was at the same time damnably clever: We must not, says he, approach the train line as long as the enemy has a telephone link. They'll catch all of us there.... He was correct, but I hated like deadly poison to engage in such trifles—cutting wires! It was no kind of job for me, but I agreed to it—all right, enough!

"So off he goes, Velfke, when evening falls, and we agree to meet up by the small woods—about five hundred meters from the line. We sit there, stuck, and wait for Velfke's signal—an owl's hoot. Then—the silence is shattered by a terrible blast. What could this mean? We strain our ears and eyes—nothing. All quiet. Soon, though, there starts tearing through the darkness one rocket after another, and all in the direction that Velfke set off in. Not good, my brothers, I think to myself—the lad has walked right into big trouble. We can't move from our spot—the area around us is all lit up like daylight. So it was decided that we should leave Marek behind to wait for Velfke, and I, along with Kivke and Aleksander, start crawling in the direction of the line. Right then it wasn't the time for talking, but each one of us was certainly thinking to himself: the way back is cut off. The enemy is on the alert and guarding the surrounding area. Not good!

"Still, a demolition man doesn't think about death, but about getting a bit of work done. We were already about two hundred meters from the line—and then rockets begin pouring over the line; so might as well dig yourself into the ground with head, life and limb. And there we are—no way ahead either!

---

1. [Smolar's note] *Thus were called the diversionary agents tasked with destroying the enemy's telegraph and telephone lines.*

"I order the gang to lie still as death. Not to move a muscle. So did they do what I said? Aleksander drags himself forward and after him, Kivke. I know my crew, once they throw themselves into something—there's nothing you can do to hold them back. I also crawl forward and I know precisely how all this will end...."

"No, it hasn't ended yet! We distinctly hear the clanging of wheels on the rails. A train is coming, puffing hard, one that is heavily loaded. Now I am once again the commander. The order is curt: 'Lay the mines, if it costs you your life!' We lie in the ditch, by the rails. Everything is ready. We're already on the track-bed, tearing into the earth tooth and nail. We can already feel the breath of the locomotive. I manage to jump down. I see that Aleksander has rolled down on the other side. Where is Kivke? ...."

Dodye fell silent, breathing fast and hard with a wheezing that sounded like the groan of a dying person. Quickly, though, a mocking grimace spread across his gloomy face:

"As you see me here—this is how I look. I alone remained. A fine commander...."

To have asked Dodye, how? what? would have been pointless. It was only later we learned that of Velfke, only pieces were found. He had been torn apart by the enemy's mine. Kivke had been blown apart together with the enemy's train by our own mine. What had become of Marek and Aleksander was for our intelligence services to find out. Meanwhile there was no news at all....

Until the notice was ready, Dodye sat with his eyes boring into the ground, his heel kicking the sand.

"Vladek, a headline in a sixteen by eight square: 'Their Lives Sacrificed, and the Combat Mission Carried Out.'"

Dodye quickly came to his feet, gratefully gave a nod with his head, and before going away quietly asked:

"When will the 'poster' be ready?"

* *
*

When Ludke had finally managed to get hold of the report from the front, the material for the first page of the forest newspaper "The Avenger" was completely ready for print. Only the third page remained. Here must be reported information about life in the enemy's rear territory. This third page was always a testimony that everywhere, even at those points most guarded by the enemy, we were there, and we knew all. We had verified information that this very page evoked the greatest of fury in the Hitler crowd of the territorial commissariat. We did have a bit of material—our spies had made a good effort. The only thing lacking was a "nail"—something "big and bold."

It remained for me to send Vladek to the headquarters of the neighboring brigade. Maybe they had something for us. Vladek had not even managed to saddle his horse when an envoy from the general arrives, saying that I must come quickly. So I jump up on Vladek's horse—I'm on my way. I arrive at headquarters—they are already there waiting for me. The chief of intelligence leads me into his dirt cave, where among several armed partisans I spot a civilian with an expression on his face as if he was sitting on a red-hot sheet of tin.

"Make yourself acquainted, Editor—you have before you the Herr Mayor of the city B."

It completely took my breath away. And my first thought was, of course: Here is the "nail," and what a nail it is! I want to go straight to the "interview," but instead of words I hear something that sounds, of all things, like the meowing of a cat . . . .

"Don't be ashamed, Herr Mayor," spoke up the intelligence chief. "Make yourself comfortable. You can free yourself of your pants, even your underpants . . . ."

I stare at him, what on earth is he saying? Then the guys tell me that the Herr Mayor had had an extremely uncomfortable journey. In the city, our spies had thrown a sack over his head and treated him without much delicacy. Outside of the city they placed him on an unsaddled horse and, not so much for comfort as for safety, they had tied Herr Mayor's feet together with a rope underneath the belly of the horse. It's no wonder therefore, that after seventy kilometers of such a journey, the Herr Mayor is not in the best of spirits. However, he follows the practical advice of the intelligence chief and quickly finds his tongue.

* *
*

When I got back to my camp late at night, the editorial cave was pitch dark. A heavy snoring bore witness to the fact that my crew had used my absence to grab a real good "snooze."

Everyone got to their feet straight away, and at dawn the paper issue was ready for print.

With Compass in Hand

Now, in happier times, the telling of it is easy. Then, however, our hearts were heavy, though we laughed along with everyone else. Did we have any choice? But inside each one of us, we felt the misfortune, the shame. One way or another—it would happen to each of us at the outset. It had a happy ending, and that is the main thing.

There came into our unit a young fellow from the ghetto. Yoshke, he was called, a barber by profession. A redhead, impetuous—a mischievous scamp. He was instantly on intimate terms with everyone. Without asking what the drill was, he straightway picked out a spot in the cave, as close as possible to the little stove. At lunchtime he was the first to run to the food pot, at the same time grabbing the best bowl—what did it matter to him, who it belonged to?

Having finished eating, he would forget to wash it out and toss it away any old place. As with every new arrival, our group would show great patience with him, make a quiet remark—and that would be the end of it. We Jews, however, did not see that this would ever stop. So we quietly began to put pressure on him—meaning, to "Be a decent human being." But he kept on with his ways.

It happens one evening in late autumn that the lad steps out of the cave. It's understandable, that a living body needs to step out! Ten minutes go by, fifteen—the boy hasn't returned. We already know that disaster has occurred, but we feign ignorance. Each one to his task—someone cleaning the rifles, another drying out his leggings by the fire, and one delousing his shirt without paying attention. Suddenly—the forest trembles with a resounding shriek:

"Guys, where are you?"

We recognize the voice; it's the little barber, and he's close by our cave—you could just about stretch out your hand and grab him by his coattails. However, the Company Commander, the always good-natured White Russian Alyentshik, is winking at us, which means: "Pretend like you don't know." At the same time, he sends out the "Little Bastard" (with such a nickname we'd crowned the twelve-year-old Vovke), and everyone takes the hint what he must do.

Soon we hear off in the distance Vovke's high-pitched voice: "Yoshke, come here, to me."

We hear Yoshke's heavy steps and panting right by the cave. Soon it falls quiet again, until Yoshke's voice bursts out in a desperate tone of voice:

"Where are you, guys?!"

And right after him, Vovke lets it be known from an opposite side of the woods, that he's actually over there . . . Again we hear Yoshke dragging his feet through the heavy snow. Every one of us, the Jewish partisans, feeling a tug at his heart, would like to make an end to this game. But it has become an accepted custom; until the company commander gives the order, no one has the right to interfere.

That night Yoshke trekked across our woods, around and around at a radius of a thousand meters, in a snow that in some places reached up to one's neck. When he finally came into our cave with Vovke, no one felt like laughing any longer. His face was dark, with white spots, signs of frostbite. He was dragging his feet as if they were stilts, so stiff had they become.

A harsh curse word tore out of one of us. It would certainly have turned into a quarrel (for a change!) had not the Commander jumped in first and half-jokingly issued the order: at the next "bombing", see to it without fail—get hold of a compass and make a gift of it to Yoshke as recognition . . . for good orientation in the woods.

The hotheaded Yoshke was ready to view the whole matter as a revolting trick. But Bashkes, the former teacher, attempted to calm him down and to console him that "it happens to every one of us."

"It's a kind of national defect. We Jews have no sense of space," Bashkes tried to explain to him, and to convince him that it came from the fact that we are urban folk; we travel all our lives on trains and tramways. In a word—flawed.

Whether or not at that moment he was able to convince Yoshke I don't know, but that Yoshke became a different person, this everybody saw. He became quieter, more settled, although from time to time he would again start squirming, begin to be agitated about this and that. Then the crew would say, "The little barber has awakened."

And indeed, it happened just as the commander had ordered—a compass appeared on Yoshke's wrist. This novelty might have gone unnoticed, were it not for the fact that after one of our battle operations, when the men had come wearily into a village, that once again inside Yoskhe "the little barber" came to life.

"I can see, lads," he said, "that all of you are dying for a drop of 'fire water.' And I see that you are also a bunch of losers. You're waiting for someone to present you with a goat, which when milked gives ninety-six proof. So you keep on waiting. For me, my insides are drying out. Well then, gang, who'll join me for a shot?"

Several spirit enthusiasts were found, who set out straight away with Yoshke across the village. The commissar sent them off with a warning: "But no stupid tricks."

We were all extremely tired. We still had an hour and a half left for rest, so we began stretching out on the floor to grab a nap.

We were awakened by the noisy return of the "spirits brigade." Slightly inebriated, they began yanking our group by the feet:

"Get up, yearning souls, time to immerse yourselves!"

And on the table appeared an entire battery of half-liters. Each new bottle pulled out was met by the members of the expedition with a resounding laugh and banter about how the owner had looked while handing over the bottle.

We were all astounded at such a rich haul. The commissar himself confronted the lads:

"You've surely stirred the hornet's nest here. You'll pay with your heads! . . . ."

Yoshke interrupted him, and began swearing with a variety of oaths that each bottle had been offered to them eagerly and with open heart, and with true hospitality.

"And had you not been such do-nothings . . . I will show you right here and now, how there will appear before your very eyes yet another half-liter."

The gang couldn't believe their eyes. Everyone urged upon Yoshke, that he should show them the trick. Yoshke spared no effort, and sent someone to summon the mistress of the hut (at the same time ordering that all bottles be cleared from the table).

In came the mistress, out of breath, and Yoshke began to deliver a speech to her:

"You see, Auntie, we don't sit around idle. This very night we gave the policeman such a whiff of powder, he'll still be sneezing when he goes to the hereafter. As you see, here before you are only heroes, true champions! Does it seem right to you, that you shouldn't offer anything to such honorable people?

The old woman began to swear that she had nothing, that she herself lived on dried potatoes. So Yoshke suddenly became deadly serious, rolled up the sleeve of his left arm, gave his compass a shake, and the needle began to move. It was silent all around. Not a breath was heard. The lads were curious to see what would happen next. Yoshke then began to emit such deep noises, that it sounded as if they were coming from his belly:

"Speak," he growled in a deep voice, looking intently at the compass, "But speak clearly: Yes or no? Aha, yes! So tell me then, where? . . . Ah . . . aha, it's clear . . . ."

The peasant woman, one could see, couldn't seem to stop squirming.

Taking a deep breath, Yoshke then turned to the peasant woman and in a milder tone gave her to understand that the partisans had invented the gadget on his wrist, and it held within it a great power—it told the pure truth.

"You see here, Auntie, this needle? It shows that there, on the other side, you've hidden a liter of moonshine. And how is it that you're not ashamed and haven't treated us with any . . . . ?"

The old woman commenced swearing that there wasn't a liter— only a half-liter in all . . . .

It wasn't long before another bottle was added to our array.

The audience rolled with laughter. Everyone began pulling from their pockets whatever they might have to accompany a drink. The guest of honor was of course Yoshke, and he led the celebration with all his enthusiasm. The boys praised him to the heavens. There were even candidates eager to make a good trade with him for his compass. Only suddenly there came, as if to spite us, the command:

"Line up! March!"

By a Special Means

Daily report of the chief of staff:

"The Sabotage group under the command of its highest-ranking member, Refoyl B., destroyed one of the enemy's freight trains, which was loaded with tanks and trucks. According to detailed intelligence, forty-six Hitlerists were killed. Train movement on the railroad line B.–M. was halted for a period of twelve hours.

"In addition, twenty-four hours later, this same group succeeded 'by a special means' in disrupting the movement of the railroad for another six hours.

"The group, headed by the senior member Refoyl B., has been nominated for government recognition."

All in the customary military wording.

No doubt the report now rests somewhere among many such reports, and it is not likely that a curious eye will linger upon it to determine what is really meant by that "special means." But among ourselves in the forest, it was talked about for a long time.

When Refoyl B. and his four saboteurs arrived in the "Safety Zone," where the enemy's bullets could no longer reach them, they still felt at their backs the conflagration of the burning train that they had derailed during the night. By the crackling sounds that carried distantly through the air, they could surmise that the train was heavily loaded, largely with ammunition.

Coming into the hamlet to see the liaison officer of the saboteur groups, Refoyl felt, along with the fatigue of a tense, difficult night, an inner discontent. Somehow, this time everything had gone off so simply, so smoothly. The Germans hadn't even managed to do a decent job of shooting up the surrounding area. Pathetic.

Having sent out the peasant to reconnoiter and determine the results of their sabotage, in order to compose the usual dispatch, the group headed for the little woods nearby to catch a nap until dusk, when one could set out into the wide world.

The group quickly fell asleep. But to Refoyl sleep did not come. Go back to the base? A depressing business. It would end up being a week, ten days of hanging around in the cave, busying themselves with housekeeping tasks—who knows, maybe even guard duty. No reason to hurry. Yet simply wandering about the area would serve no practical purpose.

Refoyl deliberated on it for some time, tossing and turning. Suddenly he burst out in quiet laughter and cheerfully began to wake up his band:

"Enough, enough snoring. Time to put together a new bit of work."

The gang looked at Refoyl with astonishment.

"What kind of work? All the mines were used up yesterday. How are we going to tear things up? With our teeth?"

"We'll tear things up, all right! We're going to village D."

The road was not a long one. The team had gotten a little rest, and the going was easier. Also buoying them up was the prospect of a good meal. Hanging back a bit from the group, Refoyl walked along engrossed in his thoughts, from time to time smiling to himself.

Having arrived at a friendly cottage in the village, Refoyl bade the mistress of the house feed his gang well. At the same time, he quietly told her daughter to go around the village and collect—as much as could be found—sour milk, sour cream; it could even be raw milk.

The lads ate well. Now came Refoyl's command:

"Drink milk, however much you can get inside you, and then a little bit more over the top!"

Immediately, Refoyl himself went out into the village and returned with a tin container, to each of whose four corners were fastened electrical wires.

In the bleary-tired gaze of his lads, Refoyl immediately recognized that the sour milk had done its work. Just at that moment, one of them tore from his spot and made a dash for the door. Refoyl stopped him and with authority pointed to the container:

"Be bold, dear brother, don't be ashamed . . . it will be of use . . . ."

Refoyl now had an additional opportunity to satisfy himself that his saboteurs were disciplined to the highest degree.

And as night began to fall, the band again set out for the same railroad line, to one of its undamaged sections. Instead of camouflaging the "electrical" container, as they usually did with a mine, they had to place it right on top, burying only the four ends of the wires in the ground.

Finished with the work, they went back to the safe farmhouse and slept there for twelve hours straight. Later, when they at last reached the liaison officer, the latter greeted them with the face of one who prepares to deliver unpleasant news.

"Somebody from our side has done some quick work here tonight. What on earth they did, only the Devil knows. No sort of mine went off, and yet the train stands there as if frozen. The railroaders say that the first train to leave after the explosion two days ago was stopped at the fifteen-kilometer point by the German patrol: 'No one can travel any farther.' Up ahead, the Germans discovered a large bizarre mechanism 'with electricity.' They were afraid to budge. They brought down a special bomb disposal unit from the city. The train has already been sitting there six hours."

* *
*

Refoyl sat down to write his account. Coming to the "electrical mine" he stopped, not knowing whether to describe it precisely (as the chief of staff always demanded), or to record it more tastefully. And this indeed is the first time when a partisan report has mentioned stopping the movement of the railway "by a special means."

No Longer an Orphan

Twice, twelve-year-old Vilik Rubezshin was left an orphan. The first time was when the band of brown-shirted murderers took over his hometown, and he was left on his own. Not knowing what had become of his parents, the underground organization in the ghetto then became his family. Vilik was our best courier. Wherever skill, agility, and quick orientation was required—that's where we would send Vilik. No matter how many times a day he needed to slip through the ghetto barricades, Vilik crept though, and not once did he fail. Whenever you needed to find someone on the "Aryan side," without even knowing the exact address, Vilik would get it done. As larger groups began to leave the ghetto for the forest, Vilik became the point man, the scout, the one that gave the all-clear to proceed.

How many times did he plead with us: "Let me go! How much longer do I have to sit here in the ghetto?" Vilik could actually have left with any of the groups. But he was very disciplined, and hated to keep on arguing. No is no. To let Vilik leave the ghetto was very hard for us.

When Vilik finally made it to the forest, in the Dzsherzshinski Detachment, the group of partisans were at first astonished at the sight of him (at twelve years old, after being in the ghetto, he still looked very much like a child): what will this kid do here with us? The detachment commander, however, already knew what Vilik had meant to us in the ghetto, and when the next set of commands was read out to the entire company, there was a special paragraph: "Consider the partisan Vilik Rubezshin to be assigned to the first detachment of the first company, and he is to be retained at the disposal of the sector commander for special assignments."

Vilik has long ago ceased to feel his loneliness. He is constantly in motion. He often goes into the ghetto and comes back punctually, meticulously fulfilling the assignment. He has already received a weapon, a sawed-off rifle that is just his size, which the band of partisans calls "V.M.P." (Vilik's machine-gun pistol).

A strong bond formed between the tall, broad-shouldered Ukrainian from Poltover region, Aleksander Borisenko, and little Vilik. Neither budges from his spot without the other. They eat together, sleep together, and together set off on battle operations.

Then Vilik was left an orphan for the second time. It just happened that this time Aleksander left without Vilik. And not far from the town of Rubezshevitsh, a hostile bullet found him. We avenged Aleksander. The enemy's nest, from which the bullet came, we destroyed down to the last brick. But it gave Vilik no peace: "Why wasn't I there with him?" Vilik was certain—he would have protected Aleksander. Vilik turned silent. An adult seriousness lay upon his boyish face. His shoulders seemed to have become broader. He's armed now from head to toe (besides a "big" rifle, he also has, as an inheritance from Aleksander, a pistol and a grenade). He's become a good horseback rider, and is considered the best scout in the company.

His group sets off for the main thoroughfare that leads to the important train station of Negoreloye. There the Hitlerists still feel very free. Vehicles cruise up and down this road, and it is difficult to find a minute to lay a mine. The group stretched out not far from the road; you had to conceal yourself and you couldn't raise your head. Vilik crept up to the road on all fours. When a light passenger car travelling before a column of freight trucks was headed very near to him, Vilik raised himself out of his hiding place to his full height, and threw a grenade into the very middle of the car. Vilik's grenade toss was a signal to the entire group of partisans. They opened fire on the rest of the vehicles and made such a "porridge" that the ambulances that came later could hardly gather together the torn-off arms and legs of the annihilated bandits.

No matter which fighting group goes off on an operation, they ask the commander to send Vilik with them, because in the partisan family Vilik is a "universal," a jack-of-all-trades. He's a mine-layer and a scout, a cavalryman and a foot soldier. By his thirteenth birthday, Vilik has racked up seven destroyed enemy trains. To sit in camp to rest up—this, for Vilik, is depressing. Therefore, you mostly find him close to the railroad, or sitting concealed somewhere in a perilous spot as he studies each move of the enemy, so as to bring back valuable intelligence for the use of the entire brigade.

It was with no light heart that the detachment commander decided to send Vilik to unoccupied "Mother Russia." And now a splendid opportunity has arrived: a Soviet airplane has landed on the partisan airstrip. How will it be in the detachment without Vilik? That doesn't matter—he should go. Let him go to the free Soviet land, take up his studies, and catch up on what he has missed these last nearly three years.

Historical Notes: *Vilik Rubezshin, also known as "Volok" and by his Russian name Vladimir Rubezhin, survived the war. According to the memorial book* We Remember Lest the World Forget, *Vilik was reunited with his parents and younger brother after the area was liberated by the Soviet army. He eventually became a construction engineer and was awarded two medals for military service as a member of the ghetto underground and as a partisan: the Order of the Patriotic War, and the Order of Glory.*

The partisan unit named in the story was the Dzerzhinsky Partisan Detachment, and the town where the Ukrainian Aleksander was killed is called Rubiezewicze in Belarussian.

Vladimir (Volik) Rubezhin – 1941

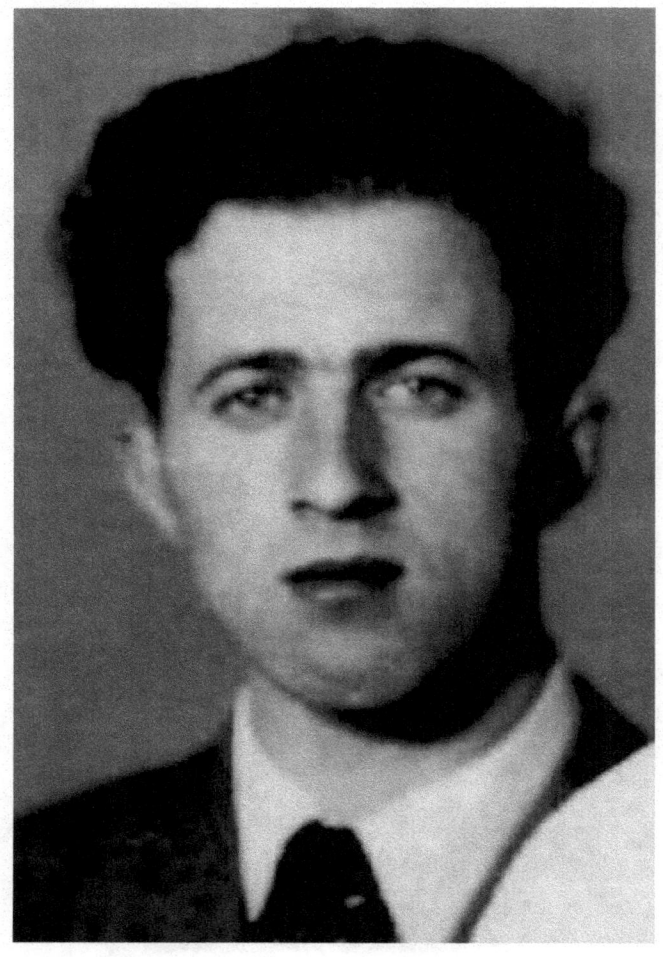

A later photo of Rubezhin captioned
"Rubezhin Vladimir Semyonovich (1929-2016) –
prisoner of the Minsk ghetto, partisan scout"

Ex Libris plates with eulogy written for Vilik by his friend Oleg Zhidovich, who was also a survivor of the Minsk ghetto.

EX LIBRIS
IN MEMORIAM
Rubezhin Vladimir Semyonovich (1929 - 2016)
Prisoner of the ghetto, partisan, reconnaissance scout
So, humbly and quietly, one by one,
the former captives leave for the unseen eternity

"Glory"
[on the Star medal]

"To the Partisan of the Great Patriotic War/USSR"
[on the round medal]

The "Deserter"

Sokher would slink about like a shadow. He could disappear unnoticed, literally from under your nose, and loom up precisely at the right second just where he happened to be needed. It was probably for that reason that the conviction arose among the forest people that he originated from the "criminal cesspool" of the "turemshtshikes," the prison inmates who had been released by the thousands from the prisons soon after the start of the war, and had flooded every road and path in the enemy's hinterland.

The people in the forest had no love for the former prisoners, and always treated them with suspicion. They especially couldn't stand Sokher because of his stubborn silence and unwillingness to reveal a word about himself, where he came from, or by which paths he had arrived there in the forest. No matter how many times someone tried to approach him with nudges and insinuations that "as a matter of fact, everything was already known about his thievish career," it would always end in the same way: Sokher's broad mouth would stretch out into a good-natured smile, and his nervously blinking eyes looked at those surrounding him in astonishment, as if to say: "Look here, how do you know all this?"

The chief of the brigade Special Detachment wouldn't take his eye off Sokher. In truth it didn't make sense that Sokher, a Jew, should have any sort of dealings with the enemy. But that his overall behavior was suspicious, well, everybody saw this. That being so, he must be caught in the act.

They would send Sokher on the most dangerous of operations, and someone in the group was always tasked with shadowing Sokher's every twist and turn, without being seen.

But the answer was always the same:

"Quite the lad—a risk-taker. He slips out from between your hands. And when he is needed, the devil himself knows from where he appears."

Anyone else in Sokher's place would have already been hailed throughout the partisan zone as a hero. They certainly would have written about him in the partisan newspaper, and who knows? Wouldn't they even have made his deeds known "upstairs," through the headquarters radio announcements? With Sokher, however, it went differently. His exploits would, as he himself did, steal by unnoticed, past the turbulent partisan daily life. When someone in the group would mention that the "felon" had once again brought a live "squealer," this was received by indifferent faces, and after a brief silence, they once again resumed their conversation about the dozens of other happenings of the day.

The news that Sokher had completely vanished from the partisan base was accepted as something self-evident. Even when someone would point out that "this fruit didn't grow in our garden," it was considered superfluous, so clear was it that Sokher had finally shown himself to be a stranger, an infiltrator, and when it was mentioned in a conversation, this was only to initiate an endless cycle of stories about the cunning tricks of the enemy, who tries to worm his way into the partisans, spy out everything, and then get out just in time.

* * *

When the chief of the Special Detachment learned that Sokher had been intercepted and brought back to the base, he jumped up from his bunk, ready to run to see the culprit. But he quickly returned to his seat, and ordered only that Sokher be confined under strict supervision. He could not, however, sit still. It was for him, the old army spy, not so much a matter of determining precisely the reasons why Sokher had fled, as it was of demonstrating to the commander that from his hands—those of the Special Detachment—not even a needle could slip out.

Of how many cutting remarks had he heard his fill from the

authorities about the Sokher affair! His contentions that Sokher seems to have been the real big fish, that one should consider a timely move of the base away from here—flew by the commander's ears. "Nonsense! He's just a good-for-nothing... he won't go far." Therefore the commander took years off the life of him, the seasoned espionage agent, on account of his "loose hands" through which real spies might indeed slip through.

But the Special Detachment chief did not, in fact, head straight for the commander's cave but turned towards the detention cell. Many minutes passed before he could, in the darkness, make out the human knot in the darkness that lay in a pool of muddy water. He bent down and tugged on the wet clothing, but he did not detect any sign of life. He picked up the body and carefully carried him off to the infirmary cave with the command:

"Summon the staff doctor, urgent!"

* * *

Levit, the detachment commissar, did not reply to the medic's message that Sokher was imploring the commissar to come to him, that he had something urgent to tell him.

There were those in the detachment who would cautiously mumble about the Jewish "clique" and that "a Jew always backs up a Jew." They didn't mean Commissar Levit. He had never given any occasion for suspicion that he went easy on the Jewish partisans. The opposite was true—he would lecture them more strictly and curse a Jew up and down more harshly, even for the smallest offense. At every opportunity he would drill into the Jewish partisans that they must be amongst the best, the most heroic: "After all, we have a double reckoning with the enemy."

Sokher's flight had hit Commissar Levit terribly hard. He had never said anything in response to the "Special's" insinuations about Sokher, but he himself knew, although Sokher had never let slip one word, that his silence, Sokher's, stemmed not from a prison cell and not from the caution of a thief.

Levit wanted to head straight for the medic's hut, even though to rush off was against his nature. Now he would know for certain that in the story of Sokher there was no sign that would confirm the "Special's" suspicion. Halfway there, he turned back to the side of the commissar's cave. As if in passing, he relayed Sokher's request to the commander.

"So go, perhaps he wants to make a deathbed confession. We do it that way. How you do it, I don't know."

When Levit came into the infirmary cave, he found Sokher on the cot, half-sitting, propped up by a pillow. His brightly animated eyes clung to the commissar's face, as if wanting to read from it whether the commissar might understand his, Sokher's, request:

"I want to live, Commissar, save me...."

"I'm not a doctor," the commissar replied with irony. He tried to shake off Sokher's eyes boring into him. "Aside from that, it seems that you're not in such bad shape."

Sokher's face resumed its former astonished expression. His wide mouth tried to stretch out into a smile, but it didn't succeed. A minute shiver went through his thin, scorched lips.

"I will certainly be put on trial, Commissar. I couldn't do anything else. I will have to go again...."

The commissar fixed his severe, penetrating gaze on him:

"What do you mean, 'I will have to'? Who do you think you are here? A law unto yourself? Men have received a lead bullet for such things, and rightly so!"

Sokher's lips had already stretched all the way out to an unnatural length. He slowly drew his wounded shoulder all the way up to his ear, and then, as if Levit's threat had nothing to do with him, he slowly repeated:

"I will have to go again...."

Whether it was from the heat that emanated from his wounded shoulder or simply from overwhelming fatigue, Sokher's eyes began to clamp shut. To Levit, it looked like at any minute his head would fall and bang itself against the side of the cot. So he carefully placed his hand underneath Sokher's head and with a towel wiped the sweat from his brow. A pair of warm, grateful eyes suddenly embraced him, and as he was already bent over, stroking the fevered brow, he remained sitting.

"Rescue her, Commissar. I've dragged her right out of the fire. She is in the village of... Not far from there are police...."

Sokher's head collapsed powerless into Levit's hands. He breathed heavily, and struggling thus, gasped out one word after another. In these words lay the "secret" of the ever-restless Sokher, who would everywhere slip by like a shadow, chasing after something that he could never find.

Her name was Miriam. It was because of her that Sokher remained as close as he could to the Germans. She had just then gone into labor. It was because of her that he was still alive and had come there to the forest. When the big Aktsye took place, they seized all three of them—brought them to the camp. And there she, Miriam, had given him no rest:

"Go! You won't be able to help us!"

So, he had gone ahead and come here. What didn't he do so it seemed to him—to be just like everybody else? And nevertheless, he was kept at a distance. He, Sokher, knew, that they suspected him of all the troubles of the world. He had no complaints. He understood: In the forest, you can only serve one master. And he had two. Had there been even one person to advise him, who would have said: "End it—there's nothing left there!"

Maybe then he would have become like everyone else. No, no one could ever have lifted from him the everlasting burden of guilt for two lives abandoned to extermination. So he ran. He knew that two deaths awaited him—one from here (as a deserter), and one from there. The bullet in his shoulder he'd gotten later, when he'd already gotten Miriam out... the child had been killed soon after he left. He brought Miriam to the village. He had to leave her there, since she couldn't have swum across the river. Our scouts had found him unconscious right on the bank. An end! Now there was one reckoning. One life... One death....

When Levit came out of the infirmary cave, Sokher lay in a deep, feverish sleep. To the nurse of many years, it seemed that his breathing had become clearer, more regular.

The First "Quintet" of the Budyonni Detachment

In the beginning, there were three—three 16-year-old lads from the ghetto: Fimke Presman, Abrashke Kaplan, and Ziamke Mitel. They were a tight group; no one could separate them. Together, the pain of having lost their mothers and fathers was eased. Together, they would certainly be able to accomplish something more quickly to quiet the burning rage against the murderers of their—Fimke's, Abrashke's and Ziamke's—parents, brothers, and sisters. Yet, as they each had no more than about sixteen years of experience under their belts, they chose V. Kravtshinski as commander of the first diversionary group of the partisan detachment named after Budyonni. Later they were joined by Yuzek Zibel, a White Russian boy, also a 16-year-old, and thus was born the quintet, the fearless destroyers of German trains and trucks. Each member of the quintet possessed qualities which together enabled them to carry out exploits that were talked about all over the region.

V. Kravtshinski's calm and deliberation was indispensable with these 16-year-old hotheads. Yuzek's wide acquaintanceship with the peasants from the surrounding area allowed them always to know precisely every step of the enemy, his battle methods and weak points. Thanks to Yuzek, the peasants would often join the quintet and together go off to blow up the railroad line. Abrashke possessed what was called "partisan shrewdness." The enemy could set himself up on all sides with guard posts, with machine gun nests, with lookout points; Abrashke would manage to crawl into the enemy's nest itself, scout it out, find out all that was needed, and vanish just in time. Ziamke's boldness was known to everyone in the detachment. Before he would set off on a risky bit of work, he would first drop in on the neighboring villages, organize meetings, converse with the peasants, and read them the reports from the front. Each time, the village would accompany Ziamke with fatherly love, sensing that from there on, Ziamke's path would take him through dangers and tremendous hardships. Everyone knew Presman to be incredibly hardheaded. If he was told, "Fimke, don't crawl in that direction—there's a huge group of Hitlerists over there," he wouldn't listen. He had to see with his own eyes if the enemy was actually so large in number, and whether one couldn't carry out a bit of "combing" of the blond beasts' heads.

It once happened that the quintet approached the large city as usual, to try their luck with a German troop train.

Along the way, they learned that six Germans were lodging overnight in the village of Kaplitshe. It would be a good harvest of "squealers"—they needed to take them alive. The quintet set off and planned out the operation so precisely that without a squeak the Hitler-bandits, together with their officer, fell into the partisans' hands, enriching the detachment with a considerable quantity of weapons and ammunition. As said, this happened incidentally. The main job had to be the train; off they headed in that direction.

At the sixteenth kilometer, the quintet decided to mine the main road, where Hitlerist cars flew back and forth. The business was a difficult one. Hitlerists lurked on all sides. Nevertheless, they managed to accomplish it. One mine had already been laid. They went up a little further, in order to set a second one—and suddenly rockets began flying. A rocket fell on Yuzek's back and burned him badly. The enemy opened automatic weapon and rifle fire from two sides. In this way, the Hitlerists intended to drive the quintet into the neighboring woods, so as to surround them and take them alive. The quintet understood this, though, and decided on the most dangerous path—to tear their way through, between the two attacking groups of the enemy.

And that's what they did. The enemy didn't notice them and continued attacking the woods. It got to the point that when one Hitlerist group began shooting into the woods, the second group assumed it was partisan fire and they began to eradicate each other.

The command of the Hitlerist garrison became agitated. It was already morning. Shooting could be heard all around, and from whom and what—no one knew. They drove off in a truck to find out what was going on, and drove right on top of the first mine that the quintet had laid that night . . . .

The local peasants reported to the headquarters staff of the Budyonni detachment. The next morning they, the peasants, were rounded up together with horses and wagons to transport the corpses. From the woods, they recovered eighteen killed, and from the main road, ten.

Linking up with the quintet was the Jewish teacher Zundl Dratfimen. It will—says he—be his birthday soon, and in honor of such an important date he wants to give a fiery salute. Normally one mine is laid; Zundl wants it to be more powerful this time. Two are laid. In a beautiful calligraphic hand (he is, after all, a teacher) he writes several "love letters" to the passengers of the oncoming German military train: "For my birthday—a gift for the Hitler travelers," and he lays them over the railroad line. A train is coming, a fancy one even, with soft seats. Certainly some "high-ranking personnel." Zundl pulls one cord, Kravtshinski with Abrashke the second, and railroad cars fly up one after the other with deafening explosions, with a brightness that lights up the entire area. The birthday celebrant, Zundl, is satisfied with his salute. Abrashke is unable to tear himself away from the spot. His ears can't get enough of the sounds of that most glorious of symphonies for a boy from the ghetto—the symphony of wails, groans, and wheezing of the shredded, dying fascists.

The entire night, the Hitlerist railroad guards shot up the area. The entire night, they brought out the dead and wounded. For the quintet this was nothing new. Coming back to the detachment, they received some news. It turned out that the intelligence had already reported the results of that explosion. Traveling on the destroyed train was a notable Hitlerist bigshot, coming from Berlin with an entire staff of "learned" bandits. All hell had broken loose among the Hitlerist people in the regional center. The German chief of the railroad hub flew in from his office. The Gestapo raged: How come the way had not been secured, when such a highly placed personage was traveling from the very bandit-headquarters in Berlin?

In battle—as in battle: there are casualties. Abrashke fell in the fight. Hitlerists had come to a nearby village. Partisans concealed themselves along the road. The oncoming Hitlerists were greeted with a ferocious hail of bullets that did away with almost all of them. Only one was left, who hid himself under the truck. When Abrashke jumped over there, the Hitler-bandit mortally wounded him.

Ziamke also perished. The fascists lurked in the village of Voltshkovitshe. They wounded the horse he was riding on. Ziamke didn't stop shooting, repelling the attacking enemy. A bullet found him. He knew: badly wounded, he could not escape from the enemy's hands. True to the commandment that he'd brought with him from the ghetto, "Never fall into the enemy's hands alive," he gave himself the last bullet in his heart.

The first "quintet" of diversionary fighters of the Budyonni Detachment was no more.

Historical Notes: *As Epstein details (2008, 205-206), the Budyonni brigade was created by escaped Minsk ghetto Jews who had been refused entry into the local partisan group and led by ghetto underground leader Nahum Feldman. They smuggled Semyon Ganzenko, a Red Army lieutenant, out of the Shirokay prisoner-of-war camp, hiding him in a barrel of garbage. Ganzenko became commander of the Budyonni otriad and Feldman the commissar; the otriad eventually grew to become a brigade.*

When the ghetto was on the point of destruction, Ganzenko supported the creation of a large "family detachment" led by Sholem Zorin, which became the 106th Detachment, or as it was better known, "Zorin's Brigade."

The Budyonni brigade contained many Jews and, as Smolar notes, "The Budyonni brigade had a strong feeling of solidarity with the ghetto. Many of the partisans had been in the ghetto themselves." Smolar also mentions the first three boys named in the story: ". . . Fimke Pressman (Tshulantchik), Abrasha Kaplan and Zyamke Mittel—who had been orphaned by a German 'action.' At [the age of] 15-16 they were proving themselves extremely helpful in the work of the resistance. Fimke, with eleven derailed troop trains to his credit, was appointed commander of the diversionary groups of the partisan detachment known as "25 Years of B.S.S.R." [Belarus Soviet Socialist Republic] (TMG 1989, 95-96).

During the establishment of the ghetto in July 1941, Smolar tells of Fimke Presman's attempt to escape: "Fifteen-year-old Fimka Pressman (later a celebrated train dynamiter) and a group his age escaped. They got as far as Smolensk, but were forced to return when they could not penetrate the enemy lines" (RM 1966, 7).

"I Have a Little Boy"

"The commander ordered that no one be admitted, no exceptions," reported the guard softly, unsure of himself, to the commissar who, as if not hearing the warning, began descending into the headquarters cave.

On the first step, the commissar suddenly came to a halt and looked pointedly at the guard, as if he wanted to hear once more the (for him) unaccustomed warning. The other, however, stood at attention, with only his eyes cast down a little ashamed, prepared to repeat once more the order he had been given.

"Well, good," the commissar answered accommodatingly, and at the same time went up to the guard, gave him a friendly clap on the back, and quickly went down into the cave. "I take responsibility for it, I'll inform the commander."

The commissar's appearance in the headquarters cave provoked no astonishment at all. On the contrary, in the commander's weary, sleep-deprived eyes a momentary brightness flashed.

"It's good that you're here, Sandler. Now you can say whether I'm correct...."

Only then did Sandler notice the woman who, hunched over with a tear-streaked, swollen face, sat to one side of the entrance. Sandler gazed at her curiously. Seeming to sense the commissar's stare, she dropped her head even lower. A difficult silence reigned in the cave for a minute. Sandler approached the commander's plank bed, sat down on the edge of it, and began to contemplate still more penetratingly the woman nearby.

"What's happened, Liube? Did your porridge get burnt for a change?"

Liube lifted her tear-filled eyes. For an instant a melancholy smile flashed in them, and then they were quickly covered once more by her heavy, swollen eyelids. A convulsive start rippled through Liube's face, sending a tremor through her entire body. Afterwards she sat immobile, as if she had dozed off.

The commander got up from his place, straightening his belt and jacket as if he were preparing to tackle an important task. He stopped near Liube, looking at her with a paternal concern, and quietly, as if to no one in particular, continued an interrupted conversation:

"They keep on killing us. Should we then help them with it? What will remain of us then? Who knows? Maybe, aside from us, there is already no one else left in the world. So that's enough—let it finally end! . . . There are no more Jews! . . . ."

The commander stood for a while with an unfocused gaze. He didn't even turn away when he felt the commissar's hand on him.

"Listen here, Commander, perhaps you will order the entire detachment to assemble and you'll give that fighting lecture of yours . . . it will certainly boost their courage . . . ."

In the commander's face, no trace remained of fatherly concern. His jaws began to twitch stubbornly, and from between his stiffly clenched teeth, he rhythmically tossed out one word at a time:

"Yes, I will indeed command it, and I will say that I, Yisroel the bricklayer, the commander of the partisan detachment 'Vengeance,' will not permit the destruction of that which should live!"

With the same resolve, but now speaking more hastily, he turned to Liube:

"That's the way it is! Don't dare to think otherwise! I won't send for the doctor now—she'll come then, when she's needed."

Liube fixed her eyes helplessly on the commander and then switched them over to the commissar, as if seeking help on his part. Sandler took in her gaze and with an ironic smile turned away from her.

"Is that all, Commander? Wouldn't you also need to set up a childbirth squad, and put out propaganda for a compulsory natural growth of our ranks?"

"Hey, I won't take your bread away from you. When it comes to propaganda, you're the expert. I rely on you," said the commander, and taking Liube by the hand, escorted her out of the cave.

"When it gets difficult for you to work in the kitchen," he advised her, "you should let me know; I will find some suitable work for you."

* *
*

As usual, this summer night at the base of the partisan detachment "Vengeance" was quiet. The senior guard paced back and forth between the tents. From time to time he halted, listened intently to the stillness of the night, and resumed pacing.

On this night, however, hardly anyone slept. The slightest sound from somewhere far off, or someone imagining he heard something, was enough to make people slip out of their huts and seek out the senior guard to see if they could learn anything.

On the base, no one talked out loud about it, but everyone knew it very well: like last summer, like two years ago, the enemy was drawing near to the forest. A blockade was coming soon. There were those who knew in precise detail that the regional headquarters had decided to take up the fight. They even knew enough to tell where each detachment would be positioned. Still others disputed this, on the assumption that it was impossible for partisans to join battle by directly assaulting the enemy's regular units; it was just a question of dividing up into smaller groups and trying, like last year, like for the last two years, to force their way through the encircling blockade.

These conjectures didn't make anyone feel better. Either way, it was small comfort for their detachment. They wouldn't be able to take on the enemy in in a fight. To break through the blockade in small groups was a matter for a combat unit, but they....

When Yisroel Mulyar had received the order from partisan headquarters to assemble in one place all the Jews, fugitives from the ghetto, who were wandering about in the area, he had no idea what to do with them all—with the women, children, old people and just plain invalids. There stood before him a congregation of Jews, looking into his eyes, willing to seize on his slightest gesture, ready even to jump into the fire. They watched his every footstep, as if they were afraid that he—their last hope—would vanish from the spot. So Yisroel thought it over and decided: What's the matter, don't they know that here one must take action?

Slowly, groupings were formed from the throng. The younger ones received weapons; the older ones took up domestic tasks. Women and children were sent to the abandoned fields to harvest the grain. Everyone did something, and their endeavors were held in high esteem by the neighboring detachments. Here's the proof: only they—as opposed to other family camps in the forests, in which lived entire villages that had fled from the Germans—received the battle designation "Partisan Detachment." And rightly so: the battle exploits of the younger ones, those who were armed, were quite impressive.

And this was all well and good in "normal" times, when night after night partisan groups would set out in pursuit of the enemy, of his transports and armaments.

But on the eve of the blockade, the "Vengeance" Detachment could sense the difference. Certainly those few who were armed could occupy a position and hold it for as long as the bullets would last. Certainly they could try to break through the blockade. But what should the rest of them do, the old people, the women and children? Divide themselves into small groups, as other detachments did, and attempt to break through? There were not enough armed fighters to be able to "cover" them. And that meant—going to certain death.

Everyone on the base knew that since early morning the entire headquarters staff was nowhere to be found, so it was likely that they would bring some very important news. No one could close their eyes to sleep, and they waited....

At daybreak the commander, the commissar, and the headquarters chief, along with their adjutants, rode in slowly, dead tired. The gathering, with their reddened, sleep-deprived eyes, stared intently at their faces, striving to pick up at least a hint that would tell them where things stood. The commissar's face was, as usual, calm, and as usual, nothing could be read from it. The headquarters chief had barely let go of the reins of his horse when he was off to the kitchen, looking in on the workshops, rummaging about in the mill and lining up the guards in formation. The commander got down slowly onto the grass near some children, and was immediately surrounded by laughter, shrieks, and play.

Someone from the group of adults came up to the children, ostensibly to wipe a child's nose, and at the same time asked:

"What's the status of things, Commander?"

"As good as it can be, my dear one," and the whole base knew immediately what this meant: we will all stay together, come what may....

The certainty *that it will be only this way* grew even stronger for everyone when that very evening, Liube gave birth to twins.

*   *
*

They left from the base as soon as it got dark. Everything went as planned. The scouts and liaisons, on horseback, were the first to set out. Afterwards, along the side roads, advancing in a half-circle to the right, set out the group headed by the commissar, protected by several dozen armed men. At the same time the group to the left, headed by the headquarters chief, also set out. Immediately after them came the center group, headed in the direction of the scouts. Leading the way was the commander. The group had not yet managed to leave the woods when the commander gave a signal to halt. His adjutant quickly went down the entire length of the line looking for Liube. He brought her back along with a woman who was helping her. The commander placed them in the row next to him, near the armed guard, took the twins in his arms, and gave the order to move on.

"Who was right, Liube," turning his head to her, the commander quietly said, and striding forward, he continued whispering, this time to himself:

"There will still be children to be raised by their mothers . . . there will still be children who will grow and be strong . . . there will be people again . . . there will be Jews . . . ."

Although no one in the long column could hear the commander's murmuring, the gnawing fear slowly faded from everyone's hearts. Their step, albeit a very cautious one, became bolder.

In front strode the commander, and in both arms, he carried the bundled-up twins, and softly, as if to put them to sleep, sang to them,

"*I have a lovely little boy,*
A little son, so fine...."

Historical Notes: *The two lines sung by the commander are from Morris Rosenfeld's famous poem "Mayn yingele," written in New York in 1887.*

By the spring of 1943, there were large numbers of ghetto refugees in partisan territory, camped out in local villages or in the woods. It was then that Sholem Zorin, then a member of the Budyonni Brigade, requested and received permission from his commander, Semyon Ganzenko, to create a family camp for those Jews who could not fight. Nahum Feldman, the brigade commissar, and Hersh Smolar, then part of another brigade, met with the commander and supported Zorin, emphasizing that the ghetto was on the brink of being destroyed. The unit, the famous 106th Detachment, consisted of both fighters and unarmed men, women, children and the elderly, grew to over six hundred people (Epstein 2008, 205-206).

Life in a partisan unit for women, already difficult, was made even more challenging by unwanted pregnancies. The responsibility for these pregnancies fell on the women, not the men. "Abortions were common and performed under trying circumstances with inadequate instruments and no medications" (Tec 2003, 322). Babies born in the forest, including those borne by women who arrived already pregnant, were typically taken away to be killed. Tec does note that there were several exceptions to this in Tuvia Bielski's detachment.

The Nurse

There was a time when a partisan would think: Better death, than to be seriously wounded. There were few medications. Also not every detachment had a doctor. A wounded person would end up suffering horribly.

But ever since Tanye came from the ghetto into the detachment, the injured, even those with the gravest wounds, no longer wished for death.

When we first met Tanye, along with several other Jewish women near a village not far from the camp, her attire—unintentionally—made us burst out laughing. She laughed along with us. The rifle with which she came into the detachment was so little suited to her entire appearance that even though we were quite used to seeing partisans in all manner of dress—in stiff and soft hats, in the styles of the different armies of the world—Tanye's "fighting" outfit compelled us to make jokes at her expense.

By profession she was a teacher. Under the Germans, she'd worked as unskilled labor in a brick factory. It was indeed from there, that she and others from the ghetto had set off without a guide "into the wide world" to reach a partisan detachment. She had some connection to medicine: she had once completed pharmacy courses. So she became the medications nurse and the doctor.

The partisans maintained that Tanye had a charmed hand. In addition to her modest knowledge of healing, Tanye possessed something more, which in the conditions of partisan life was immensely important: the devotion and love of a mother.

When the severely wounded partisan Buratshevski was finally loaded onto a Soviet airplane that had set down on our aerodrome to take him, this badly wounded fighter, to "Mother Russia," he began, in his unintelligible speech, to call out, to plead. Finally, we understood what he wanted: he was demanding that Tanye be put on the plane as well.

An enemy dum-dum bullet had destroyed Buratshevski's eye and torn out his tongue. None of us could understand his "language," only Tanye—she understood his every "word," and was our interpreter. She did not step away from the wounded patient even for a moment, spent sleepless nights and immense, effortful days, and brought it about that the despondent Buratshevski, who had more than once asked us to shoot him, began to be ashamed of his faintheartedness, and began wanting to live....

And now, this is the way of it: that which in partisan life is an everyday occurrence. An order is received to move out, cross over to a second, quite distant district. The road is a dangerous one—twice they will need to cross railway lines. Certainly they will never make it there without a fight. To take along the badly wounded is impossible. It remains that the severely wounded must be left behind, in a neighboring Jewish family camp. Tanye faces a very difficult choice: to join the fighting detachment, with all the partisans who are like family to her, with whom Tanye has passed through more than one inferno; or to remain with the wounded and sick, who need her help.

Tanye has decided: she will stay with the wounded. She will continue doing her partisan work. She will bring the wounded, sick, and mutilated partisans back to the fighting lines, so that they may, with redoubled energy, take revenge for their wounds, for their ruined health—and at the same time for the suffering that Tanye, the Jewish teacher, had to endure in the ghetto.

Historical Notes: *With the arrival of General Platon (Maj. Gen. Vasily Efimovich Chernyshev) to command the partisan forces in the Baranovichi region of Belarus, the Soviets began sending in supplies, including arms, ammunitions, clothing and medicine. They were often distributed via plane drops, but some highly guarded, secret "airports" were also created. Part of the Soviet plane's function, when they made a landing, was to transport severely wounded fighters back to unoccupied Russia. Tec described how* next to one of these airports there was a ziemlanka, a partially underground bunker built by partisans, "that housed wounded guerilla fighters who were to be flown to Moscow for medical treatment. Geler [a Bielski partisan on guard duty at the airport] says that 'One never knew if and when the plane would land. The wounded waited, some of them a long time, even a few weeks. In the ziemlanka of the wounded there were always a nurse and a doctor'" (Tec 1993, 145).

With the Enemy's Bomb

There was no command. On their own, the rustling summer dusks, with harmonica, with singing, with hearty laughter from the partisan detachment under Parkhomenko's name, became more and more subdued. Deep anxiety lay on the faces of the partisan group. Whatever someone did, they did it more thoroughly, quicker, without unnecessary debate.

"It's the eve of the 'marathon.'" Thus did the intelligence inform the partisan agents of all the far-flung surrounding administrative points, wherever the enemy's garrisons were found.

It was not the first time that the enemy had diverted entire divisions from the front in order to throw them into battle against the broad, multi-branched partisan movement; this was called a "marathon" in the partisan vernacular. To persevere and to overcome in the impending uneven fight—that was the worry of the Parkhomenko partisans, the majority of whom had just come out from the ghetto three or four months earlier.

Things suddenly became livelier when the enemy's first "greeting" arrived at the detachment. A swarm of fascist airplanes showed up over the camp. Yitzkhok Mindel just happened to be in his hut when a bomb dropped at his feet. Having fallen from the sky, it remained lying there, undetonated.

"You should say the Goyml blessing," joked the lads.

It was not the Goyml blessing that the partisan Tsukerman was thinking about as he probed and contemplated the German "gift" from all sides. He set off with Khayim Bernshteyn and Khayim Dvoskin, taking the bomb along, to send it back—"gift-wrapped," as they said—to its owners.

At the edge of the forest, the trio used the German bomb to mine the road where they expected the attack of the enemy's troops.

Cautiously, a freight truck fully loaded with Hitlerist submachine gunners began creeping its way into the woods. Scouts went up ahead, and from time to time they signaled: All good! The way is clear!

The hearts of the three partisan mine-layers began beating so rapidly that it seemed to them the enemy could hear it. Would the way really be clear for them? Shortly, the road was blocked.

The German bomb exploded and blew itself apart, together with the heads, hands, and feet of thirty Hitler bandits that had come to "carry out a marathon" in the partisan forest.

Another late fall evening. And again, the accustomed way of life in the Parkhomenko Detachment was sudden roiled. Across the vast wilderness, from one end to the other, the news spread lightning-fast: the Hitlerist collaborators—the Armia Krajowa (A.K.)—had murdered thirteen Jews, partisans from the 106th Detachment. This was a signal for the numerous partisan brigades and detachments to get a move on, and eradicate these operatives that terrorized the surrounding population.

The commanders of the Parkhomenko Detachment received news that the A.K. had firmly dug themselves in at one of the villages. A command was given: Eradicate the gang to the last man! Together with the Chapayev and Furmanov partisans, they began to encircle the bandits. But they did not allow it. They had a lot of weapons, and they sent a literal hail of bullets.

Shloyme Katsnbogen strives to find the best way to shoot; he changes his position often, edges ever closer to the enemy's side. But this doesn't do it! He grabs a horse and sets off at a gallop straight in the direction of the bandits' nest. Now he sees exactly where and who he is shooting. Totally ineffective were the warnings of Commander Siome Feygin, that it is absurd to rush at them on horseback, when the enemy is so near.

Shloyme falls, wounded. He lies stretched out, and his hands dig spasmodically into the earth. The pain is great. Tears pour from his eyes, and his head has become terribly heavy. He hears the footsteps of the enemy as they close in on him. Where does he get the strength?

He grabs his rifle and manages to drive fifteen bullets into the very thick of the assaulting Polish fascists.

Historical Notes: *Both the Parkhomenko Detachment and the 106th Detachment were well-known Jewish partisan groups. Many of the Jews who escaped from the Minsk and other local ghettos became part of this group.*

On 16 July 1944, after a parade of partisan troops in Moscow, Smolar sat around a campfire at a nearby "partisan village" with other fighters and shared this same story about killing the enemy with his own bomb (TMG 1989, 155).

The reference to the Furmanov partisans may be to a group named after writer and Red Army commissar Dimitry Furmanov. According to his book and the later film Chapayev *(1934), Furmanov fought under divisional commander Vasily Chapayev against the White Army (1919) in Turkistan during the Russian Civil War.*

The Armia Krajowa ("Home Army") was the underground resistance movement of the Polish underground, loyal to the Polish government-in-exile in London. Eventually absorbing various Polish partisan groups, by early 1944 it had some 250,000-350,000 members. A local group, the Kościuszko, formed by a local Pole, Lieutenant Kasper Miłaszewski, came to the Naliboki Forest in the summer of 1943. Smolar was personally acquainted with Miłaszewski and his otriad (as was Jewish partisan Tuvia Bielski, as they were all in the same area), and even went on a joint mission with them (TMG, 126).

After their arrival in the Naliboki forest, the Kościuszko was joined by a group of Polish officers sent by the exiled Polish government. "Some of these officers belonged to the Fascist NSZ (Narodowe Siły Zbrojne, National Armed Forces). Throughout the war the NSZ had waged multiple battles: against the Germans, the Russians, the Jews, and Poles who disagreed with them politically" (Tec 1993, 152).

Smolar writes: "One day we heard the awful news that in the nearby village of Sharkovshchisna, ten Jewish partisans of the Zorin brigade had been murdered by the cavalry unit of the Polish legion, led by Sgt. Zdzislaw Narkiewicz" (TMG, 126).

Shalom Cholawski also describes how in September 1943, when Polish units had been given orders to attack Jewish and Soviet partisan units, "Harkavi and his group, while on an operation in the Naliboki region, were attacked by a band of armed Poles. The Jewish fighting men fought bravely until the last bullet [...]. The news of the battle and the Polish betrayal spread quickly through the Naliboki forests" (Cholawski 1980, 162).

During 1943, besieged by partisan attacks, the Germans organized huge "marathons" of partisan bases, requiring them to pull multiple divisions from the front. Although Smolar consistently refers to these actions as "blockades"—writing, "The partisans called these blockades 'marathons'"—by description they were actually assaults that first encircled and then attacked partisan bases. The first marathon, with the German code name "Zauberflöte," was 17-22 April 1943: "We sustained some losses, but our brigades and detachments broke through the Nazi encirclements." In July-August 1943 came the second marathon, code name "Herman": "Fifty thousand soldiers and officers combed the Naliboki swamp, shooting and shouting as if they were on a fox hunt" (TMG, 139-140).

The Third Bridge

People were already dragging their feet like logs. It seemed that each step would be the last—one would not move on from that spot. And yet, as soon as the command "Keep going" would come, the people felt themselves gain new strength: since there was still a "Keep going," there was still a hope that they could emerge from this terrible situation. It would be worse if there was only one tiny bit of ground where they must quickly dig in, because there, near the group, the wolfish howling of the enemy's mortars would have begun.

One keeps walking, and one falls, and then one gets up again. How many weeks like this already? The blockade drags on without end. The enemy's chain around the unit becomes tighter and tighter.

By now, many would have dropped out along the way (in our present predicament, who would have looked around, to see if anyone was missing?)—no matter that death crouched on all sides; why torture themselves further? But the detachment includes the "Master of the Forest," and he never rests for a minute. He runs ahead, comes back, huddles with the commander, sniffs every bush, paws the earth; and in the hearts of the very desperate grows the hope: perhaps, in spite of everything, there is still a way out?

Until the last *Aktsye*, Bentsye Shafir had lived in the town of N. that lay on the very edge of the wilderness. When his entire family was killed and he miraculously emerged alive from the murderers' clutches, he went off to the forest. Not to the partisans—what kind of warrior would he be, he who could scarcely catch his breath? Not at his age! Instead, it was to the peasants, his neighbors, who had their hamlet in the wilderness itself, that he went, and stayed there with them. Like all peasants who lived in the vicinity of partisan bases, he also became a guide. This was because Bentsye knew the region as few others did.

His life long he had worked in the forest, traversed the length and breadth of this wilderness, knew its hidden places where no human foot before his had ever trodden.

When the blockade began, Bentsye went off to join the Jewish partisan unit. There he was known to everyone. Indeed, it was here that they crowned him "Master of the Forest."

Already in the first days of the blockade, quite a few years had fallen away from Bentsye. Nimble as a young man, he led the unit away from the Germans, right under their noses. He always found new hiding places, places it would never occur to anyone else to crawl through. But the enemy's bloodhounds would show up even there, and again Bentsye did not rest.

The situation grew worse by the day. Aside from a few biscuits, there was nothing left to eat. People were exhausted, and the shooting all around was getting closer and closer. At times it seemed that Bentsye was on the verge of collapse, done in, but unexpectedly he would start to search again, to probe, redirecting the group, and again it seemed that they had escaped.

One day as dawn broke, the group realized that they were somewhere along the edge of the wilderness. In the distance they began to see bits of open sky. Where were they now? And was it possible that there was an edge of the forest where the enemy was not present? Bentsye set off at once in that direction. Some time went by, and no Bentsye. Every shot that echoed around them might be saying that the enemy, with this one, had shot their last support and hope—Bentsye....

The old man came back tired, barely dragging his feet along. He breathed heavily and lowered himself onto the grass. His lifeless eyes were the answer to everyone's tense waiting.

"No, there are no Germans there, and there cannot be. But we won't be able to get there either. There lies the river. And on the other side is Devil's Island."

The crowd understood that their last hope had now vanished. They sat petrified, and sensed how, drop by drop, the rest of their strength was ebbing away. Only one of the youths, in a faint voice, posed the question:

"And what's there, on Devil's Island?"

Bentsye fixed a pair of bleak eyes on him, and with an old man's loquaciousness began telling about the island, where no human foot can go. One step—and the abyss draws you in. There are no trees there, only bushes, which conceal the danger lurking there for each one that tries to crawl across that accursed earth. There are birds there—multitudes of them, of all kinds. One time, in his youth, Bentsye went there with a neighbor. Oh, one needs to know how to creep through it, where to put one's foot. He, Bentsye, had traversed on foot almost the entire island. What's the use, though? How would we get there? . . . .

Bentsye remained quiet for a minute. It seemed that he had dozed off. His head dropped down heavily. Suddenly he got up from his spot and briskly strode over to the headquarters group, which lay stretched out underneath a broad pine tree.

"Chief, not everyone can be saved. Everyone who can must help themselves. To swim across that river is not easy at the best of times. Someone weakened from hunger—certainly not. But whoever wants to—let them try. I will show them how to get across Devil's Island."

The commander had not even opened his eyes while the old man spoke. He answered him in the same way, as if for no particular reason:

"Such wisdom I've already heard. Even before the raid. 'Save yourself, whoever can.' We are not Germans. We don't condemn to death women, children, old people, the sick . . . ."

The commander slowly raised himself up on one hand and remained sitting tensely in this way.

"Is it your opinion, old man, that there is no other possible solution?"

Bentsye took the commander's question, after the bitter scolding, as mocking him. So warily, he tried to answer him in the same tone:

"There is, there is. Try to borrow from Moshiach one of his two bridges—the paper one or the iron one—and on them bring the women and children across."

The commander settled on him a severe, penetrating gaze.

"Well, and is a third bridge not even a possibility? Perhaps we should try?"

* *
*

Nearer and nearer the constant gunfire sounded throughout the thick of the forest. Often human voices seemed to be audible. The people swayed, and tensely scrutinized the sudden reinvigoration in the commanders' group.

They started building the bridge in this way: from all units the strong swimmers, the young and robust, and also the very tall, were selected. Among those remaining, the unease began to grow: did this mean they would be left behind? But no one attempted to voice their doubts aloud.

Two good swimmers took Bentsye along and set out with him to the other side of the river. Those who were tall crept out into the water, as deep as they could go. The rest of the group, whoever was able to do so, began searching for long branches—as the commander had ordered. And when everything had been made ready, the commander ordered the swimmers to go out, one after the other, into the river. The weakest remained closer to shore; the stronger ones swam further out. And in this way, they stretched out in one line, lowering the branches to the riverbed in the deepest parts. And when the last command was received, one swimmer grabbed hold of the next by the foot, and across the entire width of the river there stretched a bridge made of living human bodies.

With poles in their hands for balance and, in case of emergency, to lower them into the water and lean on them, women and children began to go across the bridge. Near the commander stood a support team at the ready, prepared to switch out those who grew weak or rescue those who lost their balance.

The mortars howled around them incessantly, and blasts of automatic weapon fire, long and frequent, tore the air.

The number of partisans on the Devil's Island side steadily increased. So too increased the impatience of those in the queue awaiting their turn. On the edge of the shore stood the commander and directed each person's movement. From time to time, he noticed that someone's arms and legs were weakening and the "bridge" was beginning to break apart. He was able to send out a substitute to take their place, until that one had rested and recovered his strength. The bridge was serving its purpose, deliverance was ever nearer....

And so, when on the other side of the river, among the last to come over, the commander appeared, partisans proven in hardship and battle, ecstatic, fell on the earth in spasms of laughter. Women carried their children like banners before the commander.

And he, exhausted, with a broad smile on his emaciated face, stood leaning on someone's shoulder, and it seemed that he would fall at any moment. With his deep-sunken eyes he searched out Bentsye and quietly, but with a commander's sternness, ordered him:

"Lead on, old man!"

Historical Notes: *As mentioned in the notes for the previous tale, Smolar consistently calls the "marathons" of 1943 "blockades," although in fact they were assaults that first encircled and then attacked partisan bases, requiring several German divisions to be pulled from the front for this purpose (TMG, 139-140).*

A document by S. Shveybish (Schweibush) describes the 106th Detachment fleeing a German blockade at the Nalibokskaya Pushcha, which began on 13 July 1943 and lasted until 6 August:

"On July 13, 1943, a large blockade of the Nalibokskaya Pushcha began, which lasted until August 6. The command of the detachment managed to withdraw people from the enemy environment thanks to well-functioning reconnaissance [...]. At the same time, in order to leave light, they had to release cows and horses. The family detachment was easily vulnerable. The Nazis knew this and sought to destroy Zorin's detachment. [...].

Thus, the Jewish partisans began to prepare for the blockade and for the redeployment of the camp. But it was difficult to leave the place because of the children and the elderly [...].

"During the blockade, an island in the swamps, called Krasnaya Gorka, became a salvation. The only way to get there was through the bog. The Jewish partisans sawed the forest, made the road, crossed over the logs, then pulled them away, sawed again, made the road, and so on to the very island. [The punishers] were afraid to climb into the quagmire. After the blockade was lifted, the detachment returned to the old camp, where the cattle were again gathered [...].

"During the transition, we had to move in a chain, one after another, up to half in the water. 'Small knapsacks with things, potatoes or crackers had to be thrown into the swamp, because there was no strength to drag the children along with things'" (Schweibish 1996).

Bentsye's mention of the "Moshiach's two bridges, the paper or the iron one" is most likely an allusion to the Jewish folkloric legend about the coming of the Messiah. Various versions of this story have been told over the years. In all versions, those on the iron bridge perish, while those on the paper bridge survive—sometimes in a physical sense, sometimes in a metaphorical one. The three main versions are: 1.) The Jews are on the paper bridge, and Gentiles on the iron; 2.) The righteous are on the paper bridge, the wicked on the iron one; and 3.) The paper bridge symbolizes the Torah and all the Judaic books based on the Torah, which has enabled the Jewish people to survive. The iron bridge represents the armaments of great empires, including Rome, that despite their weapons have nevertheless perished.

The End and the Beginning

The unbroken roar of the flying Snaryad rockets was so deafening, it seemed that even if we were to shout straight into each other's ears we would still not hear each other. And so we lay dead silent, not moving a muscle.

The artillery was "at work" behind us. Close by and alongside us, as if unaware of us, crawled in furious haste entire units of regular infantry. Only now and then did a soldier creeping by look us in the eye with incredulity. By the quick gestures of his lips, we could guess that he was sending a "greeting" to our mothers, who had given the world such cowards as we were . . . .

We lay like corpses, because that was the order from the commander of our partisan unit.

The last time we saw him, our commander, he was with a group of army scouts, the first to have appeared in our woods. In haste, he issued several commands and vanished. Later, when the first Snaryads began flying in from the direction he had gone, we felt, after a moment's astonishment: It's over!

Normally it would go this way: Every time our commander went off to brigade headquarters, and especially to the regional center, we all knew he would come back with something important—a new battle order, an exploit, a mission that would give greater impetus to our constantly shifting lives. And although in the course of the years it was rare for one day to resemble the next, up until now there had still been a kind of order, even an established routine.

Now each of us felt that with the return of the commander, no trace of the lives we had led up to the present would remain. And although everyone had for many weeks spoken, told tales, and dreamed of that yearned-for day when we would abandon the earthen caves and the huts made of branches, it was precisely now, on the eve of the last command (and no one doubted that this would be the last command), that there fell upon us a painful disquiet. The anxiety increased because of the paralysis of the company, at the very moment when all around a mass of people were rapidly streaming. The anxiety increased because of the indifference of those passing by the unit, which over the years had drawn others after it, had served as an example in battle. Everyone felt an injustice was being done to us, and that there was not even anyone with whom to lodge a complaint. The commander was "over there," and there they would most certainly say to him: The time of playing partisan is over.

It seemed that our hearing was so focused, that in the surrounding racket, howling and whistling, we simultaneously heard the pounding of horses' hooves. Flying in on lathered horses came the commander along with a military man, a man scorched from sun and wind, in a dusty crumpled uniform from which it was difficult to discern whether he was an ordinary soldier or some kind of officer. Not waiting for a command, we began to get up from our places, drawing closer one to the other. Unnoticed, a half-circle formed around the riders. The army man nimbly lowered himself down to the ground and with penetrating eyes began to search among us.

"Is there anyone here, perhaps, who is my countryman? I am from Zhetl...."

His voice was hoarse. Just then, not far from us a bullet whistled by and clipped off the last words of the army man. Our group moved up closer to him, introducing ourselves as his countrymen.

People had even begun to joke at his expense and to toss adages at him from various regions. An embarrassed grimace appeared on the army man's face. The commander, making a fist, energetically jabbed towards our side. We instinctively drew back and straightened out the line. And although the commander spoke the words we had all been expecting, we were compelled to strain our ears so as not to miss a single syllable:

"It's over!"

But this referred to something entirely different. It meant that when we had before us a *Major* (the commander drew out every syllable of that word), we must forget all the partisan caprices, not joke with him as if with a buddy, but answer him in the accepted manner: Thus and thus, Comrade Major, there are none from Zhetl among us!

"There is, there is," from the line came the squeaky, thin voice of a young lad, who wanted to shout out something else but apparently seeing the stern, taut face of the commander, broke off mid-word.

"Make your way out here, lad, make your way out," the commander summoned him good-naturedly.

The young man stepped hesitantly out from the line. He placed himself next to the major, not knowing what to do with himself. One look at the commander, and the lad snapped to attention:

"It's so, Comrade Major, I am from Zhetl!"

"Is there anyone left in town? Did you know the Bergers?"

"The photographer? Certainly I knew him. There is no one left. All have perished...."

Had the woods not been shuddering non-stop, perhaps everyone would have noticed how the major gave a slight tremble. His dusty face remained stern and unmoving. And nevertheless, he suddenly became one of us, the way it would have been had he been with us all these years, hunting down those who wiped out his Zhetl.

The entire headquarters staff gathered around the major; they began to sketch something, to make calculations, to write things down. Slowly there returned to us the inquisitiveness we used to have when the commander would go off to the brigade headquarters. And now the commander's words did not ring out like an announcement of the end, that it was "all over for the partisan fighting," but like the beginning, for which we had all, during the forest years, yearned, of which we had dreamt.

Historical Notes: *Zhetl (Polish: Zdzieciol) is located 91 miles southwest of Minsk. It was occupied by the Germans on 30 June 1941 and on 22 February 1942, Jews were ordered into the Zhetl ghetto. An underground movement was organized by Alter Dvoretzky, chairman of the Zhetl Judenrat and a former lawyer. They made contact with other Jews in the* area, and with the local Soviet partisan leader. At this time there were a number of Jews who had escaped from surrounding towns hiding in the Lipichanski Forest, led by Pinya Green and Hershl Kaplinski. On 20 April 1942, Dvoretzky and six members of the ghetto underground were forced to escape to the forest after the Germans learned of their existence. Sadly, Dvoretzky was killed in an ambush by non-Jewish partisans soon after his escape.

Ultimately, the "Zheteler" partisan detachment, consisting of over 100 Jews, formed in the nearby woods. A weapon was mandatory in order to join the group. The unit included women who served in support roles as nurses, cooks, secretaries, etc. Several also took part in combat activities.

An Aktion was held 30 April 1942, in which over one thousand Jews were marched to pits outside of town and shot. A second Aktion was carried out on 6 August 1942, in which some three thousand Jews were shot and buried in three mass graves at the Jewish cemetery. Thus the ghetto was liquidated (Vershitskaya 2022).

The aforementioned Alter Dvoretzky, one of the few who "looked a little deeper and foresaw the destruction of the Jews," was the heart of the underground resistance organization. Sholem Gerling recalls him as a man who had the necessary courage and capability to conspire in dangerous conditions, keeping his work hidden not only from the German and Christian populations, but also from the majority of the Jews, who were not in agreement with his views (Kaplinski 1969, 369).

The 14-Year-Old Flagbearer

"Already? It's over?"

He knows quite well, this 14-year-old partisan Lionke Okun, that today the detachment has lined up in formation for the last time to hear the commander's orders.

Attending commanders of the forward army front-line units are speaking before the crowd, telling them: The great people's struggle against fascism draws near to its victorious conclusion. Each of you, partisans, must according to your capacity gather all your strength to bring closer the day of the great triumph.

Soon the command from headquarters arrives:

"Be prepared to march on the capital city!"

"For what?" asks softly the boy from Minsk, Lionke Okun. In the ghetto the fascists had murdered his mother and sisters. Of his father and brother, he knew nothing. Where will he return to? And what can he do there to quiet his roiling heart, to satisfy the craving for revenge for his orphanhood, for his stolen youth?

Lionke silently moved over to one side and waited until the most senior among the Soviet army officers had stepped away for a bit from the group, and pleading, turned to him:

"Take me with you . . . I can't shoot . . . ."

Lionke could actually shoot well. Even before coming into the forest, he had taken a pistol off a German officer. He has an excellent weapon at hand. So the army commander brought him along.

Lionke brought to the army his knowledge of how to lie in wait and then appear just where the enemy's troops felt quite secure. In his unit, he became a specialist in capturing "squealers."

It was the eve of the historic battle on the borders of Germany. It was imperative to find a "squealer." Lionke implores—he will bring one.

Lionke first amazed the Hitlerist he had singled out for the "squealer" with his fine German speech (he had picked this up while in the ghetto). Then he quickly gave him such a blow on the head with his automatic weapon that he lay on the ground as senseless as a log. Lionke brought him to the command point in a semi-conscious state. The command was read out before the assembled army unit, decorating Lionke Okun with an Order of Glory, Third Class.

On another occasion, on the eve of an important battle, Lionke set off with several other soldiers and brought back *two* "squealers." This time his slim childlike breast was decorated with an Order of Glory, Second Class.

During Lionke's days of fighting, there were demanding, critical moments. Especially useful to him was the hardheartedness and the cold-bloodedness he had brought with him from the partisan detachment.

The command was given to storm a point on higher ground, from which the enemy was raining down bullets. With a fierce hurrah, the army unit charged. At its head went the red battle flag. The flagbearer fell, and a second one snatched up the flag. He also fell. Lionke nimbly leaps over, sweeps the flag aloft, and moves forward with it—he is the first to arrive at the upper point.

They mustn't linger, they must pursue the enemy (he should break his back!). Lionke feels as if his strength is draining away. Cold sweat drenches him, but he runs forward with the fluttering flag, together with his attacking battle comrades. The commander shouts at Lionke: "Get down! The medics will come for you! You'll bleed to death!" Lionke doesn't stop, for greater than the pain of his wound is the joy, the immense joy of attacking and triumphing, that fills the heart of the ghetto boy.

How it was that he came to be in the hospital, Lionke doesn't remember. Soviet soldiers told him he had fainted, pressing the banner so tightly to himself that they had to pry it away from him by force.

And then the soldiers told Lionke that when he came to in the hospital for the first time, the commander was there, and had announced: The former partisan, the soldier Leonid Okun, born in 1930 in the city of Minsk, is for heroism and daring in the fight against the Hitler invaders presented with the Red Star and the Red Flag.

When the medical train on which Lionke traveled neared Minsk, his heart began to beat faster. How would it look now, his hometown, after months and years of ghetto, forest battle, and frontline? He left while still a child and he's returning a hardened man (although he is scarcely 15 years old). The enemy's bullets have pierced his body in several places. Nevertheless, his step is firm and strong on the streets of his revived hometown.

Historical Notes: *Lionke Okun (also Leonid Isaakovich Okun) was born in Minsk in 1929. He, along with his mother and sisters, was unable to evacuate when the Germans invaded and was imprisoned in the Minsk ghetto. Lionke served in the ghetto underground, but was betrayed to the authorities, and his mother, sisters and other family members, eight in total, were hanged in Jubilee Square, the site of public executions in the ghetto. After fleeing the ghetto, he fought with the 106th Detachment commanded by the Jewish partisan Sholem Zorin, then joined the Soviet Army in 1944. He was awarded the medals described in the story, becoming "the youngest Soviet solider to be twice decorated with one of the highest Soviet military honors—the Order of Glory" (Finkel 2017, 138). In a Russian interview, he briefly states that he met his father after the war. His younger brother, a Russian conscript, had been killed in 1942. Lionke immigrated to Israel in the early 1990s, and died in 2015. His video testimony ("Leonid Okon," 1993, in Russian) is available at the United States Holocaust Memorial Museum.*

Finkel tells that while in a partisan unit prior to the formation of the 106th, Lionke was charged with conducting people from the underground to the partisans. He once led out the wrong physician (who had the same name as the person targeted), angering his commander. Okun had wanted to bring his family out of the ghetto, but his commander would not even discuss it. "When Okun finally got the commander's permission, he discovered that his family was no longer alive—someone had tipped off the Germans about Okun's resistance activism and they had been executed" (Finkel 2017, 135). The formation of Jewish partisan units such as Zorin's 106th, free of antisemitism and supportive of those still trapped in the ghetto, improved the situation for Lionke and other Jewish escapees from the ghetto.

Lionke Okun with his medals
(Photo courtesy of jewmil.com)

With the Same Hands

It was terribly distressing for everyone, but there was no other choice:

We still had to stay in the forest, although the front was already tens of kilometers ahead. We still had to stay in the forest, so that the wandering, battered Hitlerist groups should not try to dig in here, take over our bases, and from here terrorize the area. We also had to stay in order to recover all the mines that we ourselves had laid in various places. Now they threatened with death the innocent peasants who came into the forest after firewood, after berries.

Certainly, all of this was understandable. But to sit without a stitch of work, at a time when other units had left for the front, or had taken over full authority in their districts and were shaking things up—this was unbearable. There were partisans who could find no rest, hanging around without knowing what to do. Their movements became sluggish, their faces dull, grubby. Things would become a little livelier when the scouts would signal that they had come upon the tracks of plodding Germans. A shootout would begin—you'd think the sky had opened up. They hammered away at each other for no particular reason, and the entire matter quickly came to seem like the thrashing of wildlife flushed out during the hunt, rather than the conduct of a normal battle. But this did not happen often.

Generally, when dusk fell, we would gather in a circle and start expressing—more often and more loudly as time passed—our dissatisfaction with headquarters, which had left us stewing in our own juices. It was already so far gone that when the headquarters chief raised a battle alarm in the middle of the night, it was painfully long before the group was up and out of their burrows. Some of them even had to be dragged out by their feet and brought into formation.

On this particular night no one felt like lying down to sleep, though there remained many hours before the march. The headquarters chief informed us of the command from Central that the company should set out for headquarters, where all the best partisan brigades would be assembled. There we would learn what each of us needed to do next. At once the accumulated lethargy fell away from the partisans. Our movements became quicker. From the merest hint, we seized on each command from headquarters, and with special zeal took pains to carry it out precisely. We began cleaning our clothes, giving ourselves a thorough wash-up. There soon sprung up entire barber "establishments," and we all helped each other to achieve a respectable appearance, though everyone knew that the road ahead was long and that more than one person would fall by the wayside.

At the last minute, when everything that could be loaded onto the wagons was already packed and we had begun collapsing the caves so the Germans couldn't move into them, a heavy, crushing stillness fell upon everyone. We grasped then that never again would we return to these places, which had sheltered us like a home and protected us like a mother when mortal danger lay waiting at every step. Silently, almost one by one, we set out from the woods. When we approached a village, we began to draw closer together, to form rows and knock out a military tread on the dusty country roads. Everywhere peasants came out, greeting and saying farewell to old acquaintances, calling many by name or by partisan nickname.

In the last row, heavily loaded with a rucksack, came the senior diversionary agent, Shloyme Strikher. On his fierce countenance there was no visible sign of emotion at this parting from old places and friends. Only now and then, when the greeters would call "Be well, Shliomke," would a grimace appear on his face, the closest he came to a smile.

Shloyme Strikher was returning over the same road on which, two years earlier, he had come here from the ghetto; the same road that had led him, the senior diversionary agent, scores of times to the trains and highways of the enemy. He was returning to a home that was no longer a home, where no one awaited him. He dragged the feet that had been so nimble on missions and assignments, and were now so heavy that they scarcely moved.

But before he reached the great river on whose opposite bank the train station stood, Shloyme Strikher was called aside by the commander. In the peasant cottage that he entered, he encountered, along with members of the unit headquarters, several army officers.

"Here he is, the main culprit," the commander presented him, in dead seriousness, to the officers.

Shloyme stood stunned, not knowing where to focus his squinting eyes. Now, at the very end, to be suddenly accused! What was going on here?

A rather small, lively captain led him out of his perplexity:
"How did you bring down the bridge?"
"The bridge? Which one?"
The officers meant the bridge on the nearby river.

Shloyme was back in his element. He told them of the first battle for the bridge, of how it was blown up almost by their bare hands, and then about the second battle for the same bridge when the Germans had rebuilt it—this time with rifles and grenades against machine guns and automatic weapons. The last bridge was destroyed with explosives. That time, the work was very neatly done—no bridge would ever stand there again . . . .

"Actually, that is what this is all about," a prematurely gray captain interrupted him in mid-sentence. "There will be a bridge again soon. And you will help with it."

* *
*

Now it was the second day that the unit had been transformed into a work brigade. Men waded half-naked into the water, and the differences between soldier and partisan were erased. They tried to outpace each other: the military men in order to show their expertise in building even when the partisans had left no trace of any bridge, the partisans in order to make it back in time to the partisans' assembly place.

It was hard at first for Shloyme Strikher to pick up the work tools in his hands, the same hands that up to now had been accustomed to breaking things apart, blowing things up, destroying. The axe did not serve, and the plane jammed too often. He was bathed in sweat, and he, a carpenter, son of a carpenter, must be encouraged and consoled by the brash captain that, never mind, it will work out, you have to get used to it. Certainly demolition was easier . . . .

It wasn't the sweat in his eyes—it was resentment of the officer that set Shloyme's teeth on edge. Because what did he know, that front-line officer, about how easy it was to destroy, with bare hands and teeth and fingernails, that sturdy bridge? What did he know about Shloyme's blazing hate, which had transformed him from the builder into one with an unquenchable drive to destroy and lay waste?

And the stronger grew his resentment of the officer (who tried like a big brother to encourage and motivate him)—the more skilled and agile did his hands become in finishing one section of the bridge after another. And it seemed that the deep-set furrows on Shloyme's face smoothed out and became narrower, as if they were at the point of disappearing.

* *
*

Appended to the partisan unit's battle report was the account of the first reconstructed bridge.

Historical Notes: *Despite all the hardships of life in the forests, it was difficult for the partisans to leave their comrades and the now-familiar woodland environment, and to return to a world that had been horrendously and irrevocably changed, if not utterly destroyed. When it was time for Cholawski to leave the forest, he writes, "We found it hard to accept the fact that we were to leave the forests. The sufferings, dangers, and battles that we had experienced in the forests now bound us to these dark masses. The forests had once terrified us, but now they blessed us with the feeling of security. We had spent two years less two weeks in the forests—more than seven hundred days and nights! Here in the forest, hope still whispered; the outside promised uncertainty and loneliness" (Cholawski 1980, 177).*

Appendix

TRANSLATOR'S NOTE:

This appendix consists of my translation of the Warsaw Ghetto memoir written in Yiddish by Natan (Nosn) Smolar, Hersh Smolar's older brother. The bilingual version of my translation also includes the Yiddish of the original handwritten manuscript. Nosn's memoir is not part of any of Hersh Smolar's books, but I felt that Smolar would want it to be included for modern readers. Clearly devoted to his brother, Smolar dedicated both the 1948 and 1952 versions of his text to Nosn, describing him as "my brother and friend, Nosn, who died a hero's death in the Warsaw ghetto". Like his brother Hersh, Nosn was an active part of ghetto resistance, and he was also a trusted friend of Emanuel Ringelblum; this memoir forms part of Ringelblum's archive. It is dated 10 December 1942. Like so many others, Nosn and his family died a cruel, unprovoked, and unjust death.

Born in Zambrów, Poland, in 1901, he was a graduate of the teachers' college in Vilnius, Lithuania and a member of the Left Poalei Tsion party. As a Yiddish teacher in the Warsaw ghetto and a member of Emanuel Ringelblum's underground Warsaw ghetto archive, known as the Oyneg Shabes project, Nosn was so highly valued by Emanuel Ringelblum that he was one of a core group of Jews whom Ringelblum intended to rescue after having left the ghetto (Kassow 2007, 359).

As part of the ghetto Left Poalei Tsion party, Nosn Smolar taught Yiddish at the party's Borochov school, which also housed a children's soup kitchen and served as the site of the party underground press and hiding place for Oyneg Shabes (Kassow, 119). He ran the school along with fellow teachers and party members Feige Hertslich and Israel Lichtenstein. He was killed sometime on or after 18 April 1943, the eve of the ghetto uprising.

In December 1942, Nosn Smolar contributed to Ringelblum's Oyneg Shabes project this eulogy to his three-year-old daughter, Ninkele, who had been deported in August. In it he recalled the happiness of her third birthday, and his grief at her loss: "And today there is no more Ninkele, nor her mother, nor my sister Etl [...] At three years old she already knew what a raid was, what a Jewish policeman—snatcher of old people and small children—was; she already knew enough to hate them" (Smolar, N. 1942, 1).

Nosn's testimony now resides at the Emanuel Ringelblum Jewish Historical Institute (Żydowski Instytut Historyczny im. Emanuela Ringelbluma) in Warsaw, Poland. It exists in two forms: the original eleven-page handwritten Yiddish manuscript (pages 10 and 11 are misnumbered), and an incomplete typed Yiddish version transcribed by an unknown author at the Żydowski Instytut Historyczny sometime after the end of WWII. The handwritten version and permission to use images of both copies was provided by the Żydowski Instytut Historyczny im. Emanuela Ringelbluma. The typed version was generously provided by Hersh Smolar's heirs.

10 December 1942

Dedicated to the Shining Memory
of My Dear Little Only Daughter Ninkele

It was not so long ago—the eleventh of July, 1942, when we celebrated your birthday—that you turned three years old; our good, close friends—Folye with her Vishke, Fele with Vladke and Nelush, Felke Faynlikht with her Rutke, and more and more.[1] How many playthings, mechanical toys, noisy, playful, had piled up, how much children's joy, noise, tumult; and with a glass of tea, we wished with all our heart that you might live to see your fourth birthday in better circumstances. And today—no more Ninkele, her mother is also no longer; and no longer my sister Etl,[2] who was so filled with pride for Ninkele's progress, her wit, who marveled so at her intelligence, her initiative in games. At three years old Ninkele already knew what a raid[3] was, what a Jewish

---

1. The identities and correct name spellings of these people is unknown. The Jewish Historical Institute (Żydowski Instytut Historyczny) in Warsaw notes that Fela is "[p]erhaps Fejga (Fela) Herclich-Blit (ca. 1902–1943), activist of Poalej Syjon-Lewica, teacher from the school at Ward Street 68" (Note 985). (ARG t33 212 406).
2. Etl is listed as Etel Smolar (p. 3033) in the *Memory of Treblinka* database; her date of death is given as July 1942. An Estera Smolar (p. 3032) is also listed with a date of death as June 1942, but there is a note that says this date is incorrect. No listing was found for Ninkel: https://memoryoftreblinka.org/people_db/p3033/; https://memoryoftreblinka.org/people_db/p3032/ respectively.
3. The original word in the text is *blokade* ("blockade"). Nosn Smolar seems to use the term "blockade" just as Hersh Smolar does in his stories: rather than a conventional military blockade, it describes an assault that first encircles and then, attacking and killing, rounds people up. In the case of the Warsaw ghetto, it was used mainly for deportations. I have substituted the word "raid"

policeman—snatcher of old people and small children—was; she already knew enough to hate them.

To my sister in New York—1468 Leland Avenue, Bronx—Pauline (in Yiddish "Peshe") Daytshman: in case I do not survive, let whoever has the opportunity send you this small thing (for a thousand worse things happened), this saga of your family.

Your brother Noske

Our dear mother began the family's travails of Job in Zambrów, at the end of July, 1941. A week earlier she, the determined one, had risked her life, and for the price of a gold watch (from father's wedding gifts) set off for Białystok on perilous roads to find out if her children were still alive. She took with her a small bag of crackers and a little kasha and oil for her children, because at that time Jews in Białystok were afraid to go out in the street to pick up a little food. She located only me and Etl, who had gone from Zambrów to Białystok on the second day of the war. Esther had immediately left Białystok on the first day and there had been no news at all about her; Hershl had left the second day and was stuck somewhere among the villains. I had received news about him from somewhere in the Baranovich area. My mother went back that same night; altogether she was with us for one day. About a week later, the band of German murderers entered Zambrów, called together and chased into the street the entire town—some fifteen hundred people, old and young, men and women with small children, whom they brought to the Czyżew area, dragged into the woods where wide ditches had already been dug, and there did away with all of them. The news reached us in Białystok three weeks later. We, especially Etl—our mother's youngest daughter, so timid, so pampered—took it very hard.

After a time, first I and later Etl left Białystok and came to Warsaw. How happy Etl was when I succeeded in setting her up to work as a teacher in an orphanage. She devoted so much of her heart to the

---

for "blockade" throughout this document, as it more accurately describes this type of assault. Also see the *Historical Notes* in "With the Enemy's Bomb."

children—how often she sat for hours seeking the perfect little song or game for them. She loved them as a mother loves her own children. Today the children are no more; Etl is no more.

I've become a little sidetracked from the chronology of the story—forgive me, sister.

Some time later, before the start of the "relocation" (that's the name the Germans gave to the mass murder of Jews),[4] there began the prelude, the prologue to the tragedy: shootings started in the streets, a car would drive by and shoot Jewish passers-by for no reason. After that an organized nocturnal mass shooting: some fifty Jews dragged out of their homes, led several houses further down, ordered to keep walking, and taken down from behind. Later a fresh group of a hundred people were pulled out of the detention houses and shot; a proclamation reported this as a punishment, because they had not obeyed the decrees of the German authorities and had even resisted them. And again, tens and hundreds—one murder after another. Rumors went out, each one darker than the last, that we would be driven out of Warsaw, somewhere beyond the city. No one believed it—how would it be possible to expel us all from Warsaw, such an ir vee'ym beyisroel, a Jewish capital, a city of four hundred thousand Jews? They reasoned to themselves that certainly it would happen to the homeless, to those who had arrived here from other places, but by no means to those born here. Until it began.

Placards were posted—all Warsaw Jews "except" . . . and if only there hadn't been all the "excepts," perhaps there wouldn't have been so many victims.[5] Perhaps some sort of self-defense would have been

---

4. The "Great Deportation" (Nazi code name *Grossaktion*—"Great Action") began on 22 July 1942, with the Germans ordering that 6,000 Jews be deported to Treblinka each day. When it finally ended on 12 September, over 250,000 Jews from the Warsaw ghetto had been sent to their deaths at Treblinka. A smaller deportation was also carried out on 18 January 1943, and was met with violence from the ghetto underground resistance.

5. Kassow writes, "The Germans cunningly announced that a number of categories would be exempt from deportation: employees of the Judenrat and the Aleynhilf, those with work in German enterprises, and others who

mounted, it wouldn't have come to such a shameful end, that over three hundred thousand Jews, among them tens of thousands young and healthy, should be led like sheep to the slaughter.

"Except," was stipulated in the announcements, "except" for all of those who work in the shops[6], in the community institutions, in the supply establishments, social institutions (the Jewish Aid Committee, CENTOS, OZ), craftsmen's unions and others. Yes, and they may all take under their protection their wives and children, who are not required to be deported.

People began running helter-skelter, until the Jewish police succeeded in expelling from the refugee sites all the poorest of the recent arrivals, and from the houses the poor people who didn't have the means to buy their way out. Ninety percent already had vouchers attesting that they belonged to the privileged categories and did not have to be deported.

I too—as I was employed by the community, I was placed in a shop—I became a woodworker, and after much pain and effort my wife and child were also taken under the protection of the shop, although my wife herself was also employed by the community.

Since a panic had already set in that the J.A.C (Jewish Aid Committee) authorization passes were no longer recognized, that at any minute the community passes would also no longer be recognized, the "shop" was a hundred-percent good-luck amulet by comparison. And to confirm the rumors, it was pointed out that first one and then a second person from the J.A.C., from the community, was snatched up regardless of their passes. When I finally received my registration card with the red stamp from the SS, I finally felt completely secure,

---

were gainfully employed. [...] The Resettlement Squad faced the mammoth task of deporting hundreds of thousands of people, set Jew against Jew and fooled the Jews into believing that a document or a job would actually save them" (Kassow 2007, 301).

6. "Shops" were production posts (*platsuvkes*), consisting of small and medium-sized factories under private German ownership that provided for Nazi needs.

and also assured for my family, for whom I'd received a special certificate for family members. Even so, to reassure myself further, I took my wife and child into the factory with me, as did hundreds of other shopworkers. In the courtyard of our factory (at 30 Genshe[7]) they were seated far from any evil eye and sat there during the day, and when the murdering devils—the Jewish police, the German SS gangs and their Ukrainian, Lithuanian, and Latvian lackeys—finished their day's work, we would go off into our houses to spend the night, often not getting undressed due to the continuous night shootings and wild rumors about nighttime pogroms.

And one day not long after, the shop-amulet became impure, and to my misfortune, our shop was the first to have this shield swept away. This was on a Friday, the 7th of August, a total of seventeen days after the start of the mass murder. The women with their children and the elderly were, as they were every day, seated deep inside the courtyard, invisible to the outside world, when the SS with the Ukrainians came rushing in from behind, through the fence of a neighboring courtyard. The crowd was remarkably calm; everyone was told to get up, line themselves up, and walk towards the gate, where their documents would just be checked. All of them had documents, so they remained calm, they came up to the gate; what documents? Which documents? Keep walking—and whoever dared to say a word in opposition got the whips and riding crops straight in their faces; a few were shot, and everybody keeps walking. We, the men, didn't even know that this had happened, because at the factory we had to go full steam ahead. Everyone had to be at their station. They didn't even look inside the factory; they detained them all and led them off to the Umschlagplatz[8] (the modern Golgotha from which they were brought in railroad cars

---

7. Polish "Gęsia" street before WWII. It was later renamed Mordechaja Anielewicza Street after one of the leaders of the Warsaw Ghetto Uprising.
8. A walled-off area of the western side of the Warszawa (Warsaw) Gdańska freight train station adjacent to the ghetto, from which some 300,000 Jews were deported to the Treblinka II extermination center.

to the slaughter-site of Treblinka, where the mass executions took place by gas and shooting).

In vain I threw myself after them, like a wounded animal in a cage. I ran to the Umschlagplatz, and paid to find out whether my wife Esther and Ninkele were there. Then I sent Dr. R.[9] with money, a lot of money, to bribe the police. I sent our own factory police; I managed to learn that they had successfully avoided the first transport of 6,000 people that had left at eleven o'clock that morning, but by force and blows they were driven out of their hiding places when the second transport left that same day. Nothing could have helped. With a child in your arms, it was impossible to avoid that wretched fate. I received news that my wife had been seen with Ninkele in her red coat, on their way to the railroad cars. I continued making futile efforts, telephoning someone who had business connections with the Treblinka camp stewards. He answered that he could do nothing, that in that place there was only wholesale death (he too, was later shot). And from then on, the light of the shops was gone. The gang had seized not only family members, but wantonly, regardless of who had or didn't have a shop-pass, just whoever they pleased.

Now frequent raids on the shops began. It was done like this: A few SS men entered; immediately after them the Ukrainians spread out through the factory, and then the Jewish police. Everyone is ordered to come down to the courtyard. Women and children conceal themselves. The Ukrainians search. With money, watches, or other jewelry, people buy them off, but often others come after them and drive the people out of their hiding places. In the courtyard, an SS-nik walks by with his whip and drags out this one and that one, who are told to go off to one side—that is, to death. Whoever doesn't move quickly enough gets lashed with the whip or, as happened with us in several cases, shot on the spot. The selected ones move around, attempting to run across to the row of those remaining; the Jewish

---

9. [Footnote 993, translation mine] "Probably Emanuel Ringelblum" (ARG t33 212 406).

police do their duty faithfully, they don't let you—until[10] you bribe them, like the Ukrainians, with jewelry or a few hundred zlotys. Many manage for the moment to save themselves in this way. During the raid, some hide in the already established hideouts, thanks to which a remnant of the women still remained. At the same time as the raids in the shop there is a raid in the residence block of the shop, from which all those who haven't managed either to conceal themselves or to bribe the Ukrainians are being dragged out. And this was how I managed—partly by hiding during the raids, partly by pure luck—to stay alive until this day (10/XII).[11]

On the night of the 5th to the 6th of September, a new piece of bad news arrived: all shops, all "platsuvkes"[12] that worked for the Germans on the Aryan side, were to be dissolved. Everyone must leave their residences by ten o'clock in the morning, Sunday, the 6th of September, and come to a few designated streets (Miłą, Lubeckiego, Stawki)[13]; there a new selection of all the workers will take place, and those who make it through the selection will afterwards be able to return to their places. I live on Miłą Street, and the morning of 6 September I stood at my window and watched. No pen, no image is adequate to render the nightmare image of that morning.[14]

Tens of thousands of dejected, despairing, unwashed faces, mothers

---

10. This word *khibe* is missing from the typed manuscript.
11. (10/XII) refers to the date of the original manuscript: December 10, 1942.
12. [Translation mine] "In the Warsaw ghetto, the term used for places where Jewish forced laborers were deployed beyond the walls" [on the Aryan side] (Klaus-Peter 2014, 425).
13. Original parentheses ended after "place."
14. Kassow tells us "The nightmare culminated on September 6, the first day of the "cauldron." Early that day all Jews who remained in the ghetto were ordered to assemble in a small area of streets adjoining the Umschlagplatz. For three days a massive selection took place, as employees of each shop and workplace had to march past SS officers who would decide who would die and who would receive a precious "work number." The Germans planned to issue only thirty-five thousand numbers. The SS separated children from parents and wives from husbands" (Kassow 2007, 303).

with children on their shoulders, wailing children torn away from their mothers, masses and masses of people pacing back and forth, helplessness in their eyes. And they kept coming, and more followed. And then the selection takes place, and some of them go back, and again the greater part of the thousands are led off to the Umschlagplatz.

A thousand and one tales of misery are being told by those who survived those days. Who can really express it, though? Every word is a reliving of the tragedy. Our selection took place only on the fourth day—Wednesday. Every day we waited, as one awaits the Messiah, for our boss—the German, Henzel—and finally came the good news: our shop will remain, 500 men may stay, and since after so many roundups there are fewer than 500 left, it seems like everyone can stay. To be on the safe side, the older people, women, and children should hide themselves; the rest can confidently present themselves. We waited an entire day for the SS personnel, who were to carry out the "selektsye," and just at six in the evening they appeared, like a maddened tempest, like a swarm of locusts. Leading the charge was he himself—the murderer, Brandt.[15] With bloodshot eyes and a hoarse cry, they quickly, quickly took to their "work."

Shrewd entrepreneurs at the factory had seen how to exploit the climate of fear and hammered out brass tags with the inscription "O.B.W."—Ostdeutsche Bautischlerei Werkstätte[16]—with numbers, and sold them for three zlotys. Men called these tags "dog tags," and actually bought them up, as if they were true amulets, against any trouble that might come, even though they were not guaranteed. In order to make a show of importance, they didn't sell the tags to women. The SS men did accept the tags as important documents, and whoever didn't have such a tag was condemned. With wild cries,

---

15. SS Untersturmfuhrer Karl George Brandt, a German police officer who was one of the lead perpetrators of the 1942 deportations. He was extremely feared for his brutality, sadistic behavior and ruthlessness.
16. The "East German carpentry workshop" on 30 Gęsia Street where Smolar worked, was owned by Aleksander Landau, an active supporter of both the Oyneg Shabes project and the ghetto resistance.

with whips and riding crops and Big Man Brandt with a board in his hand, they separated us into two camps. Each of the condemned was beaten with brutal blows; twice Brandt's board broke over the backs and heads of those not moving fast enough. Blood gushed from those running across, condemned to death. And in order to incite more rage, or perhaps to justify his revolting behavior in the eyes of the German civilian shop bosses, with every blow he shrieked: "It's not enough, not enough for you, we've bled for three years already because of the Jews, because of you the German people suffer."

Among the hundreds of men and women was Etl, too—my sister. Her children's home had already been taken to the sacrificial altar. I had taken her into the factory as my wife, managed to receive a factory pass for her, a registration card with the SS stamp, all done properly, and she lived with me. She went confidently to the selection. She had no doubt that she would make it through. Who else if not her, a twenty-two-year-old—young, blood-and-milk fresh, pretty. All the more since the quota for the factory workers had not been exceeded. The SS quickly separated out those with the dog tags and told them to go back to the factory. Then they carried out a vicious raid in the residences, dragged out some who were hidden there, and afterwards led them all away, straight to the railroad cars, and there was no more trace of Etl.

Then more raids, internal selections and abductions took place. Meanwhile I remained there.

About what happened to my sister Khane and her daughter Beltshe, I know nothing. I only know that in Zambrów, in November, the same thing happened. There the executions were carried out in Czerwony Bór Forest[17]; I've no news of them.

---

17. The SS carried out executions in the Czerwony Bór Forest beginning in July 1941, with the largest mass murder taking place in August 1941. The Zambrów ghetto was liquidated 1-2 November 1942 (Megargee 2012, 984-985).

First page of original manuscript from Oyneg Shabes archive

10 דעצעמבער 1942.

דעם ליבטיקן אנדענק פון מיין טייער איינציק מעטטעל
נינקעלע גאווידטמאן

אם נים לאנג - דעם 11 יולי 1942 האבן מיר געפייערט דיין געבורטס-טאג
- 3 יארעלעך איז דיר געוואון, נאנטע - גוטע פריינד - פאליע מיט איר ווישקען
פעלע מיט וולאדקען און נעלושען, פעלקע מיינליכס מיט איר רוטקען און נאך
און נאך. וויפל שפיל-צייגן באוועגלעכע, רוישיקע, שפילנדיקע האט זיך אנגע-
זאמלט וויפל קינדערשע פרייד, געלויב, געמוטל. און ביי א גלעזל טיי דיר
און גאנצען הארץ געוואונטשט דעם 4-טן געבורטס-טאג איך פרייערע באדינגונגען
צו דערלעבן. און היינס - נישטא מער נינקעלע, נישטא אויך איר מאמע, נישטא
אויך מיין שוועסטער עטל, וואס האט אזוי געקוואלן פון איר אנטוויקלונג,
פון אירע חכמות, אזוי באוונדערט איר אינטעליגענץ, איניציאטיוו אין שפיל-
רייען. שוין אין אס די 3-יאריקע האט געוואוסט, וואס הייסט פלאקארד, וואס הייסט
א יידישער פאליציאנט - באפער פון אלפע לייט און קליינע קינדער, שוין זי
האט געוואוסט זיי פיינט צו האבן.

שוועסטער מיינע אין ניו-יארק - בראנקס לעלונק עוועניו 1468 - פאלי
/היימיש פעשע/ דייטשמאן; טאמער איך וועל נישט קליבן, זאל מען עס דיר
איבערשיקן ווער עס וועט האבן די מעגלעכקייט די קליינינקע /וו-של ס'זיי געוויט
מארגעקומען טדיינס מאל שרעקלעכערע זאכן/ מגילה פון דיין משפחה.
דיין ברודער נחמן

אנגעהויבן דעם פאסיליען-איוב האט אונזער טייערע מאמע אין זאמבראוו
סוף יולי 1941. נאך א וואך פרייער האט זי זיך די הארציקע אייגענעטמעלט דאס

Bibliography

Abbreviations for books by Hersh Smolar
[Written in Yiddish as *Smoliar*]:

FMG	*Fun minsker geto*
RM	*Resistance in Minsk*
SY	*Sovetishe yidn hinter geto-tsoymen*
TMG	*The Minsk Ghetto: Soviet-Jewish Partisans Against the Nazis*
VBK	*Vu bistsu khaver Sidorov?*

American Association of Professors of Yiddish. *Yiddish*. Flushing: Queens College Press, 1985.

Arendt, Hannah. *The Jew as Pariah: Jewish Identity and Politics in the Modern Age*. New York: Grove Press, 1978. Quoted in David Kaposi, "To Judge or Not to Judge: The Clash of Perspectives in the Scholem-Arendt Exchange" *Holocaust Studies, 14(1):93-116* (June 2008), 242-243.

Cholawski, Shalom. *Soldiers From the Ghetto*. San Diego: A. S. Barnes and Co., Inc., 1980.

Epstein, Barbara. *The Minsk Ghetto 1941-1943: Jewish Resistance and Soviet Internationalism*. Berkeley and Los Angeles: University of California Press, 2008.

Finkel, Evgeny. *Ordinary Jews: Choice and Survival during the Holocaust*. Princeton: Princeton University Press, 2017.

Fogel, Joshua. "Khayim Aleksandrovitsh," Yiddish Leksikon (blog), June 29, 2014, yleksikon.blogspot.com/2014/06/khayem-aleksandrovitsh.html.

Friedrich, Klaus-Peter, ed. *Polen: Generalgouvernement August 1941-1945, Band 9.* München (Munich): Oldenbourg Verlag, 2014.

Goldkorn, Yitshak. *Heymishe un fremde literarishe etyudn.* Buenos Aires: Farlag Sevivah, 1973.

Gutman, Israel. *Resistance: The Warsaw Ghetto Uprising.* Boston: Houghton Mifflin, 1994.

Guy, David. *Moving Through the Years Gone By... One Family's Chronicle.* New York: Self-published, 2016.

Heller, Binem. *Sefer Lukov: geheylikt der khorev-gevorener kehile.* Tel Aviv: Irgun yots'e Lukov be-Yisrael, 1968.

Hiemstra-Kuperus, Els, and Lex Heerma van Vos, Editors. *The Ashgate Companion to the History of Textile Workers, 1650–2000.* London and New York: Routledge, 2016.

Kaganovitsh, Moshe. *Di milkhome fun di Yidishe partizaner in mizrekh-Eyrope.* (2 vols.) Buenos Aires: Tsentral-farband fun Poylishe Yidn in Argentine, 1956.

Kaplan, Shabtai, et al., *Lebn un umkum fun Olshan.* Tel Aviv: Irgun Yotzej Olshan, 1965.

Kaplinski, Baruch, ed. Pinkes Zhetl: *tsum 15-tn yortog nokh dem groyzamen khurbn fun unzder gevezener heym.* Tel Aviv: Irgun 'ole-Zhetl in Yisrael, 1957.

Kassow, Samuel. *Who will write our history?* New York: Vintage Books, 2007.

Lanzmann, Claude, dir. *Claude Lanzmann Shoah Collection, interview with Hersh Smolar, conducted in Yiddish.* 1979/1985, United States Holocaust Memorial Museum: Film | Accession Number: 1996.166 | RG Number: RG-60.5038 | Film ID: 3377 3:30 min. (Event: September or October 1979; Production: 1985)

Megargee, Geoffrey, General Editor, et al. *Encyclopedia of Camps and Ghettos, 1933-1945 / Vol. 2, part A,* "Ghettos in German-occupied Eastern Europe." Bloomington: Indiana University Press, 2012.

Organization of Partisans, Underground Fighters and Ghetto Rebels. Heiblum, Reuven. (Hebrew ראובן הייבלום). Accessed June 20, 2022, on ThePartisans.org; website unavailable at time of publication.

Perechodnik, Calel. *Am I A Murderer?: Testament Of A Jewish Ghetto*

Policeman. Edited and translated by Frank Fox. Boulder: Westview Press, 1996.

Person, Katarzyna. *Assimilated Jews in the Warsaw Ghetto, 1940-1943*. Syracuse: Syracuse University Press, 2014.

Porter, Jack Nusan. *Jewish Partisans of the Soviet Union during World War II*. Brookline: Cherry Orchard Books, 2021.

Roth, Cecil, and Geoffrey Wigoder, eds. *Encyclopaedia Judaica, Vol. 12*. New York: Macmillan Company, 1971.

Rudling, Anders. "The Khatyn Massacre in Belorussia: A Historical Controversy Revisited." In *Holocaust and Genocide Studies*, Volume 26, Issue 1 (Spring 2012): 29-58.

Skirda, Alexandre. *Nestor Makhno—Anarchy's Cossack: The Struggle for Free Soviets in the Ukraine 1917-1921*, translated by Paul Sharkey. Edinburgh: AK Press, 2004.

Smolar, Hersh, translated from Yiddish by Max Rosenfeld. *The Minsk Ghetto: Soviet-Jewish Partisans Against the Nazis*. New York: Holocaust Library, 1989.

Smolar (Published in Yiddish as "Smoliar"), Hersh. *Fun minsker geto*. Moscow: Melukhe-Farlag "Der Emes," 1946. Published in Russian as *Mstiteli Geto* (Moscow: Der Emes, 1947. Published in English as *Resistance in Minsk*, translated by Hyman J. Lewbin).

— *Resistance in Minsk*. English translation of *Fun minsker geto* by Hyman J. Lewbin. Oakland: Judah L. Magnes Memorial Museum, 1966.

— *Sovetishe yidn hinter geto-tsoymen*. Tel Aviv: Farlag I. L. Peretz, 1985. (Republished in English as *The Minsk Ghetto: Soviet-Jewish Partisans Against the Nazis*)

— *Vu bistsu khaver Sidorov?* Tel Aviv: Farlag I. L. Peretz, 1975.

Smolar, Natan (Published in Yiddish as "Nosn Smoliar"). "*Dem likhtikn ondenk fun mayn tayer eyntsik tekhterl Ninkelen gevidmet*" ("Dedicated to the shining memory of my dear little only daughter Ninkele"). Warsaw: Żydowski Instytut Historyczny (Emanuel Ringelblum Jewish Historical Institute). Letter dated 10 December 1942 (Courtesy of E. Smolar).

Schweibush, S. [also S. Shveybish]. "Jewish Family Partisan Details of

S. Zorin." Bulletin of the Jewish University in Moscow, No. 3 (13), 1996. Archival copy April 3, 2015. Accessed July 11, 2022: jhist-org.translate.goog//shoa/russia/partiz.htm?_x_tr_sch=http&_x_tr_sl=ru&_x_tr_tl=en&_x_tr_hl=en&_x_tr_pto=sc [article read in English machine translation].

Strauss-Marko, Shlomo. *Poylishe Yidn in di velder, driter band, Kamf un nekome*. Tel Aviv: H. Leyvik Farlag, 1983.

Tec, Nechama. *Defiance: The Bielski Partisans*. New York and Oxford: Oxford University Press, 1993.

Resilience and Courage: Women, Men and the Holocaust. New Haven and London: Yale University Press, 2003.

Vershitskaya, Tamara. "Zdzieciol (Zhetel)." *Holocaust Encyclopedia*. United States Holocaust Memorial Museum, undated. Accessed June 20, 2022: encyclopedia.ushmm.org/content/en/article/zdzieciol-zhetel.

Żydowski Instytut Historyczny. *Archiwum Ringelbluma. Getto warszawskie* "ARG t33 ARG II 212 (Ring. II/219/1)." Obtained August 2, 2022.

— *Archiwum Ringelbluma. Getto warszawskie* "255.Ring.II/201." Obtained August 2, 2022.

ACKNOWLEDGEMENTS

This book simply would not have been possible without years of dedicated help from three people: my two teachers, Leybl Botwinik and Norman Buder, and my editor, Catherine Madsen. My non-native-speaking, book-learnt Yiddish was no match for the complexity and agility of Smolar's, and my teachers spent hours helping me understand what he was saying; Catherine aided in the translations as well. Her intelligence, expressiveness and humor were a match for Smolar's, and she helped elevate my translations to his level. All three of them are skilled writers and translators in their own right, and I truly enjoyed every minute spent with them. I'm a better writer and translator for it.

Essential to this project was the support of Smolar's family. His sons and grandson not only gave me permission to publish this translation, but provided me with additional historical material and cheered me on throughout a quite lengthy timeline.

I am very grateful to Solon Beinfeld for his always patient responses to the dozens of emails I sent him concerning difficult passages in this book. His knowledge of Yiddish, Eastern European history, and Russian were invaluable. I am honored and so pleased that he wrote the introduction to this text.

Thank you to the Lupyan family—the children of Tsilye Botvinik ("The Czech Rifle")—for the background information and photos. Thank you to Elena Maximova once again, for the Russian translations.

Thank you to my husband, Jon, my son, Rory, and Joseph Boucher, for lending their military expertise to this project. Smolar thinks and writes like a fighter, and there are many battles in this book. They gave me the vocabulary I needed.

I am so grateful to my cats Oyskuk, Bashe and Khonen for their unfailing love and support. *Olekho hasholem*, Oyskuk—I miss you more than words can say.

ABOUT THE AUTHOR

Hersh Smolar (1905-1993) was a Polish and Soviet Yiddish writer and editor. He was born in Zambrów, Poland. Smolar was exposed at a young age to the socialist and revolutionary ideas of Russian Jews in the years before World War I and the Russian Revolution. He attended primary school until he was 11 years old, when he began working, and quickly began his revolutionary activities. A leader of the local arm of the Jewish Socialist Youth Association (1918-1920), he then belonged to the Zambrów revolutionary committee formed during Soviet occupation.

Smolar fled to Soviet Russia in 1921, and two years later was admitted to the Yiddish department at the Communist University for the Peoples of the West, a university run by Comintern. He served as a Comintern agent in Poland from 1928 to 1939, was twice arrested, and spent six years in prison. After World War II began, he fled to Białystok and worked as editor of the Communist newspaper *Byalistoker shtern* (Białystok Star). A founding member of the resistance in the Minsk ghetto, Smolar later became commissar of a Soviet partisan group operating in the Naliboki forest. His memoir of this time, *Fun Minsker geto* (From the Minsk Ghetto), was published in Moscow in 1946.

After the war, Smolar and his family returned to Poland, writing and editing in Yiddish newspapers. The rise of anti-Semitism in Soviet Russia and his sons' involvement in dissident activities eventually led to his leaving for Israel in 1971. In addition to his Minsk ghetto memoir and *Yidn on gele lates* (Jews Without Yellow Stars), he published four further volumes of his memoirs, covering most of his life: in 1975 *Vu bistu khaver Sidorov?* (Where are You, Comrade Sidorov?); in 1978 *Fun ineveynik* (From Inside); in 1982 *Af der letster pozitsye mit der letster hofenung* (At the Last Position with the Last Hope); and in 1985 *Sovetishe yidn hinter geto-tsoymen* (Soviet Jews behind Ghetto Walls; 1985).

ABOUT THE TRANSLATOR

Ruth Murphy's translations have appeared in *Metamorphoses, Pakn Treger,* and the *Yiddish in Translation* section of the Yiddish Book Center's website. *A review of her translation The J. Abrams Book: The Life and Work of an Exceptional Personality, was published in the Jewish Review of Books.* She has also published Yiddish-to-Spanish translations online, including a short story by Jacob Gordin. Her bilingual Yiddish-English text, *The Canvas and Other Stories by Salomea Perl,* was published by Ben Yehuda Press in 2021. Upcoming works include *Binele* by B. Y. Bialostotzky and the play *Khasye di yesoyme* by Jacob Gordin.

ABOUT THE EDITOR

Catherine Madsen learned Yiddish while working at the Yiddish Book Center, where she served as Bibliographer and contributing editor to the Center's magazine, *Pakn Treger*. Her essays have also appeared in *Cross Currents, Tikkun, Parnassus, The Sun,* and many other journals. She is the author of three books: *The Bones Reassemble: Reconstituting Liturgical Speech*; *In Medias Res: Liturgy for the Estranged*; and a novel, *A Portable Egypt*.

Recent books from *Ben Yehuda Press*

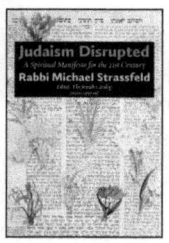

Judaism Disrupted: A Spiritual Manifesto for the 21st Century by Rabbi Michael Strassfeld. "I can't remember the last time I felt pulled to underline a book constantly as I was reading it, but *Judaism Disrupted* is exactly that intellectual, spiritual and personal adventure. You will find yourself nodding, wrestling, and hoping to hold on to so many of its ideas and challenges. Rabbi Strassfeld reframes a Torah that demands breakage, reimagination, and ownership." —Abigail Pogrebin, author, *My Jewish Year: 18 Holidays, One Wondering Jew*.

The Way of Torah and the Path of Dharma: Intersections between Judaism and the Religions of India by Rabbi Daniel Polish. "A whirlwind religious tourist visit to the diversity of Indian religions: Sikh, Jain, Buddhist, and Hindu, led by an experienced congregational rabbi with much experience in interfaith and in teaching world religions." —Rabbi Alan Brill, author of *Rabbi on the Ganges: A Jewish Hindu-Encounter*.

Liberating Your Passover Seder: An Anthology Beyond The Freedom Seder. Edited by Rabbi Arthur O. Waskow and Rabbi Phyllis O. Berman. This volume tells the history of the Freedom Seder and retells the origin of subsequent new haggadahs, including those focusing on Jewish-Palestinian reconciliation, environmental concerns, feminist and LGBT struggles, and the Covid-19 pandemic of 2020.

Duets on Psalms: Drawing New Meaning from Ancient Words by Rabbis Elie Spitz & Jack Riemer. "Two of Judaism's most inspirational teachers, offer a lifetime of insights on the Bible's most inspired book." — Rabbi Joseph Telushkin, author of *Jewish Literacy*. "This illuminating work is a literary journey filled with faith, wisdom, hope, healing, meaning and inspiration." —Rabbi Naomi Levy, author of *Einstein and the Rabbi*.

Weaving Prayer: An Analytical and Spiritual Commentary on the Jewish Prayer Book by Rabbi Jeffrey Hoffman. "This engaging and erudite volume transforms the prayer experience. Not only is it of considerable intellectual interest to learn the history of prayers—how, when, and why they were composed—but this new knowledge will significantly help a person pray with intention (*kavanah*). I plan to keep this volume right next to my siddur." —Rabbi Judith Hauptman, author of *Rereading the Rabbis: A Woman's Voice*.

Renew Our Hearts: A Siddur for Shabbat Day edited by Rabbi Rachel Barenblat. From the creator of *The Velveteen Rabbi's Haggadah*, a new siddur for the day of Shabbat. *Renew Our Hearts* balances tradition with innovation, featuring liturgy for morning (*Shacharit* and a renewing approach to *Musaf*), the afternoon (*Mincha*), and evening (*Ma'ariv* and *Havdalah*), along with curated works of poetry, art and new liturgies from across the breadth of Jewish spiritual life. Every word of Hebrew is paired with transliteration and with clear, pray-able English translation.

Forty Arguments for the Sake of Heaven: Why the Most Vital Controversies in Jewish Intellectual History Still Matter by Rabbi Shmuly Yanklowitz. Hillel vs. Shammai, Ayn Rand vs. Karl Marx, Tamar Ross vs. Judith Plaskow... but also Abraham vs. God, and God vs. the angels! Movements debate each other: Reform versus Orthodoxy, one- two- and zero-state solutions to the Israeli-Palestinian conflict, gun rights versus gun control in the United States. Rabbi Yanklowitz presents difficult and often heated disagreements with fairness and empathy, helping us consider our own truths in a pluralistic Jewish landscape.

Recent books from *Ben Yehuda Press*

Reaching for Comfort: What I Saw, What I Learned, and How I Blew it Training as a Pastoral Counselor by Sherri Mandell. In 2004, Sherri Mandell won the National Jewish Book award for *The Blessing of the Broken Heart*, which told of her grief and initial mourning after her 13-year-old son Koby was brutally murdered. Years later, with her pain still undiminished, Sherri trains to help others as a pioneering pastoral counselor in Israeli hospitals. "What a blessing to witness Mandell's and her patients' resilience!" —Rabbi Dayle Friedman, editor, *Jewish Pastoral Care: A Practical Guide from Traditional and Contemporary Sources.*

Heroes with Chutzpah: 101 True Tales of Jewish Trailblazers, Changemakers & Rebels by Rabbi Deborah Bodin Cohen and Rabbi Kerry Olitzky. Readers ages 8 to 14 will meet Jewish changemakers from the recent past and present, who challenged the status quo in the arts, sciences, social justice, sports and politics, from David Ben-Gurion and Jonas Salk to Sarah Silverman and Douglas Emhoff. "Simply stunning. You would want this book on your coffee table, though the stories will take the express lane to your soul." —Rabbi Jeff Salkin.

Just Jewish: How to Engage Millennials and Build a Vibrant Jewish Future by Rabbi Dan Horwitz. Drawing on his experience launching The Well, an inclusive Jewish community for young adults in Metro Detroit, Rabbi Horwitz shares proven techniques ready to be adopted by the Jewish world's myriad organizations, touching on everything from branding to fundraising to programmatic approaches to relationship development, and more. "This book will shape the conversation as to how we think about the Jewish future." —Rabbi Elliot Cosgrove, editor, *Jewish Theology in Our Time.*

Put Your Money Where Your Soul Is: Jewish Wisdom to Transform Your Investments for Good by Rabbi Jacob Siegel. "An intellectual delight. It offers a cornucopia of good ideas, institutions, and advisers. These can ease the transition for institutions and individuals from pure profit nature investing to deploying one's capital to repair the world, lift up the poor, and aid the needy and vulnerable. The sources alone—ranging from the Bible, Talmud, and codes to contemporary economics and sophisticated financial reporting—are worth the price of admission." —Rabbi Irving "Yitz" Greenberg.

Why Israel (and its Future) Matters: Letters of a Liberal Rabbi to the Next Generation by Rabbi John Rosove. Presented in the form of a series of letters to his children, Rabbi Rosove makes the case for Israel — and for liberal American Jewish engagement with the Jewish state. "A must-read!" —Isaac Herzog, President of Israel. "This thoughtful and passionate book reminds us that commitment to Israel and to social justice are essential components of a healthy Jewish identity." —Yossi Klein Halevi, author, *Letters to My Palestinian Neighbor.*

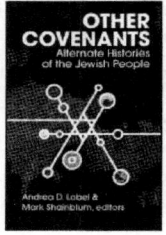

Other Covenants: Alternate Histories of the Jewish People by Rabbi Andrea D. Lobel & Mark Shainblum. In *Other Covenants*, you'll meet Israeli astronauts trying to save a doomed space shuttle, a Jewish community's faith challenged by the unstoppable return of their own undead, a Jewish science fiction writer in a world of Zeppelins and magic, an adult Anne Frank, an entire genre of Jewish martial arts movies, a Nazi dystopia where Judaism refuses to die, and many more. Nominated for two Sidewise Awards for Alternate History.

www.ingramcontent.com/pod-product-compliance
Lightning Source LLC
Chambersburg PA
CBHW070550160426
43199CB00014B/2449